How to Improve Your Prayer Life

Though this book is designed for group study, it is also intended for your personal enjoyment and spiritual growth. A leader's guide is available from your local bookstore or from your publisher.

Copyright 1987
Beacon Hill Press of Kansas City
Kansas City, Missouri
Printed in the United States of America
ISBN: 083-411-1594

Stephen M. Miller
Editor

Molly Mitchell
Lisa Norris
Editorial Assistants

Jack Mottweiler
Chairman

David Holdren
Stephen M. Miller
Carl Pierce
Gene Van Note
Lyle Williams
Editorial Committee

Contents

Chapter 1

How to Know if You're Praying Sincerely

by Stephen M. Miller

Background Scripture: Matthew 6:5-13

SOME INSINCERE PRAYERS are easier to spot than a dead leopard on the altar.

Take the mealtime prayer of my grade school buddy, Bill. "Rub-a-dub-dub. Thanks for the grub. Yea, God."

Then there's the Nazarene pastor's wife who was asked to say grace at the church fellowship luncheon. "Thanks a bunch as we munch on this lunch." Her husband politely asked her to please try again, this time with a real prayer.

Some insincere prayers, though, aren't quite as obvious—at least to us. (God can spot them right off.) In fact, some insincere prayers can seem as pious as all get-out.

If that's so, how can we tell the difference between an insincere prayer we may be praying, and one that is sincere?

Fortunately, there are some telltale marks of both. These aren't all sure-fire indications of insincerity or sincerity. But they're at least clues you need to look for as you evaluate your prayer life.

Marks of Insincere Prayer

1. Prepackaged prayers can be insincere.

The Jews of Christ's time had a warehouse of carefully crafted prayers for all occasions. They had a prayer for before the meal, one for after the meal, one for entering a city, one for leaving a city. They even had a prayer to say over new furniture.

So no matter what the circumstance, the Jew probably had a memorized prayer up his sleeve. Don't get me wrong; I'm sure many people prayed these prayers from the depths of their heart. But most of us know how easy it is for memorized prayers to become rote and downright meaningless. They can become a string of words we wave in the wind with almost no effort.

If you would have joined me around my family dinner table a few years ago, you would have heard one of my stock prayers. "Father, thank You for this food. Bless it to our bodies. For we ask it in Christ's name. Amen." If you practice, you can learn to say it in five seconds, without taking your mind off the sweet aroma of roast beef, mashed potatoes, and corn on the cob slobbered with butter.

With hardly any trouble at all we can turn any prayer into a packaged, formal prayer. We've even done it to the Lord's Prayer, which Christ gave His disciples as an example of a prayer off the top of the heart—something opposite of a prayer from the cobwebs of our memory or the dried ink of a giant printing press.

When I was a youngster in a family of five kids, each night we'd have family devotions. We'd all kneel by a piece of furniture in the living room, and one of us would serve as the pray-er that night. Then we would all join together in the Lord's Prayer, as a kind of benediction. It sounds like a good idea at first—one you might be using. I know it's one tradition I continued after I got married.

But somewhere along the line, I realized it took heavy-duty concentration to actually think about its meaning while I prayed it. It was just too easy to slip from brain-in-gear to brain-in-neutral. That's when we stopped using it regularly. Now, when we pray it once in a while at the end of our prayer time, it is meaningful and lovely.

2. *Long, elegant prayers can be insincere.*

If you want someone to pray a long public prayer that's so word-perfect and holy sounding it's sure to get the Holy Spirit's rubber stamp without any editing, don't call on me. I stumble over my words when I pray—even in private. And that used to bother me.

I used to feel like the pastor's wife I know of who told

her husband, "Oh, I'd give anything if I could pray like you." But you know what she was really saying? She was saying, "I wish I could pray so well people would think I had prayer down to an art, from so much practice. Then they would know I'm holy." Or she could have been saying, "If I could put words together like you, God would be more apt to listen."

The first paraphrase represents a vain pastor's wife. The second reveals a woman who has a warped idea of what God is like. God doesn't expect everyone to pray like they could make a living at it. How could He? He hasn't given everyone the gift of public speaking. All God expects from us in prayer is that we speak from the heart, and trust Him for the answer.

A little English boy had the right idea about the relative unimportance of words in prayer. The lad was praying, "A, B, C, D, E, F, G, . . ." when a gentleman walked by and asked what he was doing. "I don't know what to ask for, or how to ask, so I thought I would say the letters to God a good many times and ask Him to put them together the right way."

When we talk with God, we don't need to preoccupy ourselves with creating elegant words that will tickle His ears, or with long prayers that will convince Him of our concern. The Lord's Prayer, Christ's model of simplicity and sincerity, is only 52 words in my NIV translation. And two verses before it, in Matthew 6:7, Jesus clearly says, "When you pray, do not keep on babbling like pagans, for they think they will be heard because of their many words."

3. Self-promoting prayers are insincere.

This mark of an insincere prayer is a lot like the one I've just mentioned. That's because self-promotion in prayer is commonly done through lengthy, beautiful prayers offered in public places.

In Matthew 6:5, Jesus said, "When you pray, do not be like the hypocrites, for they love to pray standing in the synagogues and on the street corners to be seen by men."

Many of us know that pious Muslims will stop each day, face Mecca, and pray. But did you know that in Christ's time, pious Jews did much the same? Three times a day— morning (often at 9 A.M.), noon, and evening (often at 3 P.M.)—they would stop in their tracks and have devotions. This included a set of 18 prepackaged prayers, most of which are lovely. The fifth prayer says: "Bring us back to Thy law, O our Father; bring us back, O King, to Thy service; bring us back to Thee by true repentance. Praised be Thou, O Lord, who dost accept our repentance."

When it came time to pray each day, it wasn't too hard for the Jew to plan it so he would be standing on the top step of a busy walkway, or on a downtown street corner. Some- times these folk would stand for hours, repeating scriptures, saying the set of 18 prayers, and adding their own sermonic prayers for all to hear.

When we pray today, we're wise to strip our prayers of self-promotion. As a teenage Christian, I still remember the men's prayer meeting in which I delivered a carefully re- hearsed prayer that traced the steps of Jesus from Geth- semane to Calvary to glory. I actually practiced it the night before the meeting. Now there are times when we need to do some advance thinking about a public prayer we're to speak on behalf of a congregation. But I wasn't so much interested that Saturday morning with organizing my thoughts as I was in protecting myself from looking like a spiritual wimp in the middle of a bunch of prayer samurai.

After the prayer time, an older fellow put his arm around me and said, "Steve, that was a beautiful prayer." And I agreed. But as I think back on it, I imagine the Holy Spirit must have done some serious rewrite on my prayer. The revised version could well have gone something like: "This young man loves You, though he still loves himself a little too much. Be patient; I'll work with him on it."

4. Established times and places for prayer can spawn insincerity.

You've probably been advised that it's a wise thing to set a regular time to read Scripture and pray. And that's a good idea because if you don't, the demands of our busy world can rob you of your quiet time with God.

But limiting ourselves to set times is a bit like limiting ourselves to prepackaged prayers. It becomes too easy to slip out of manual and into automatic. New Testament scholar William Barclay tells the story of a Muslim who had a knife drawn and was chasing an enemy. In the middle of the chase, a Muslim crier called out the news it was time for prayer. The knife-wielding Muslim stopped, unrolled his prayer mat, knelt, raced through his prayer, then rose to continue his murderous chase.

Now we're not likely to chase someone with a butcher knife after our devotions (unless our spouse suddenly arrives home with a dent in the new car). But we can get to the point where we associate prayer almost exclusively with church services, mealtime, and devotions. But prayer is a day-long, ongoing dialogue with God: "Lord, it's 10 A.M. and my wife's meeting with the pastor about a sticky wicket personnel problem in the nursery. Guide them to a good solution." "Father, my work has just been revised beyond recognition. Help me to maintain a healthy attitude."

Marks of Sincere Prayer

1. Private prayer can be the most sincere.

That's not to say public prayer is insincere. It's just that when we pray alone, there's no need to strike our best pose.

When I'm praying in front of others, even if it's just my wife, I'm very conscious of the fact that ears are tuned in my direction. And frankly, that's the way it should be. While we do need to pray from the heart, we also need to know that others can be hurt or helped by what we say.

Without trying to sound too mysterious, there are some things I talk to God about privately that I don't even share

9

with my wife. But when I'm alone with God, there is no one who can be hurt by my honesty, no weakness to hide, no ego to protect.

We can and should be sincere in public prayer. But for me, achieving sincerity in public prayer is like zigzagging down a busy city street, trying to avoid the obstacles. Private prayer is a straight shot on the interstate.

2. Sincere prayers are directed to God.

Have you ever fantasized while you prayed privately, imagining that your words were being spoken before a large and prestigious gathering?

I have. About the only time I've ever waxed eloquent in my prayers was in such moments of imagination. And then, I wasn't praying to God. I was performing for an imagined audience.

Other times I've found myself praying to a real audience. Those were times I caught myself talking to the people instead of to God. I was saying things like: "He sent His Son to die for us." "Our Lord helps us in difficult situations." Third person phrases like these are dead giveaways that we've left the land of prayer and strayed into a sermon or a testimony. And this is even more obvious if we drop our voice a couple octaves and pray in sermonic-sounding tones.

The Lord's Prayer is an excellent example of what it's like to pray directly to God. Here God is addressed in the first person, as though He's standing right before us as we speak. In those moments of prayer, we talk to Him about our hopes for the Kingdom, and our needs of the day.

3. There is no such thing as a sincere prayer without honesty.

One of the most obvious marks of sincerity in prayer is honesty. In fact, the two words—*sincerity* and *honesty*—are so closely related they could almost share the same definition. God wants us to talk with Him about all our feelings, both the good ones and the bad ones.

One of my most profound spiritual encounters came after I "dumped" on God. It was an unbearably hot August evening in Kansas City. I was a few courses away from completing a master's program in seminary, after working on it for over two years. In addition, I had been holding down a full-time job. So I was exhausted. I was one day away from taking my oral, comprehensive exam in which three professors would grill me for a couple of hours on all I learned in seminary. Since the failure rate was nearly 40 percent for the last batch of seniors, I was nervous. To make matters worse, my girlfriend of one year had just traded me in for a bald-headed insurance salesman. So I was depressed.

I'm glad God has broad shoulders, for He needed them that night. As I lay on the couch, in my small apartment, I told God exactly what I thought of all this. And I told Him I wasn't thinking too highly of Him either. In fact, I bawled Him out for deserting me when I needed Him most. "Where are You? Where's that joy, that peace, that sense of Your presence?" In nothing less than anger and desperation, I grabbed *The Living Bible,* opened it at random, and dared God with something like, "OK, let's see what You have to say for Yourself!"

God knows when we need something beyond the natural, beyond mere coincidence. My finger fell on verse 27 of Isaiah 40. Here's what it says through the end of the chapter.

> O Jacob, O Israel, how can you say that the Lord doesn't see your troubles and isn't being fair? Don't you yet understand? Don't you know by now that the everlasting God, the Creator of the farthest parts of the earth, never grows faint or weary? No one can fathom the depths of his understanding. He gives power to the tired and worn out, and strength to the weak. Even the youths shall be exhausted and the young men will all give up. But they that wait upon the Lord shall renew their strength. They shall mount up with wings like eagles; they shall run and not be weary; they shall walk and not faint.

11

On that couch, I wept as the presence of God filled the tiny living room.

The next day, I took the exam. Not only did I pass, I was so relaxed it seemed to bother one of the professors. That night, I called home to give Mom the news. I had been telling my troubles to her during those stressful days. She was 800 miles away, and though I didn't think she could do much to help me, she was a caring heart who shared my pain. So I wanted her to share my joy as well.

"Before I go, Mom, I want to read you the passage of scripture God gave me last night."

I had just started to read when she interrupted me. "Son, I read those same verses late last night. And I prayed, 'If only I could give these to my boy.'"

She couldn't talk anymore.

"I love you," she whispered. "Good-bye."

The tears came once more.

Whenever I can't seem to sense the presence of God, whenever I wonder if He'll ever respond to my sincere and honest plea, I remember this touchstone in my life. That night of nights when He visited a tired, nervous, and lonely seminary student to remind me that He's always but a breath away.

4. Sincere prayers can be simple.

You don't have to hold a master's degree or a doctorate to talk to God. Sometimes I wonder if this much education tends to hinder our talks with God.

Consider how simple is the prayer Jesus taught His disciples. "Give us our food again today, as usual, and forgive us our sins, just as we have forgiven those who have sinned against us" (Matthew 6:11-12, TLB).

I believe God hears even the prayers of children. In fact, I wouldn't be surprised if children had a higher percentage of answered prayer than us adults. Kids are so honest and direct in their prayers.

When I was growing up, my dad wasn't a Christian. But

he wanted to be. The trouble was, he couldn't quit smoking, and for some reason he felt he had to give up smoking before he could turn his life over to Christ.

For years my two brothers, two sisters, Mom, and I privately prayed for Dad. Once, when we kids, Mom, and Dad were kneeling at a family altar in the living room, little Louise—my younger sister—prayed in her toddler drawl, "Peas help Daddy 'top pokin' dem cigalettes."

Eventually, Dad accepted Christ—even though the cigarette habit had not released its grip. But something extraordinary happened that day. No longer could he smoke without getting nauseated. That was one time in his life Dad was glad to get sick to his stomach.

We've referred to just a few of the clues that can alert us to insincerity in prayer. And we've focused on some of the characteristics of sincere prayer. But in the end, there is no sure-fire checklist; the answer to whether or not we are sincere in our prayer life must come from the heart of the individual. And this answer will be as tough or as easy to reach as is the answer to, "How can I know if I love God?"

For as Samuel Coleridge wrote in "The Rime of the Ancient Mariner": "He prayeth best who loveth best."

Chapter 2

Questions You Always Wanted to Ask

by Arnold Prater

Background Scripture: Romans 8:28, 31, 35-39

GOD PREFERS BOLD PRAYERS to humble prayers.

At any rate, it would appear that way to me since so many people today insist on asking God for something in one breath, then on thanking Him for it in the next breath.

This leads us to the first of the great problems of prayer with which we want to deal.

Should we claim a promise and "thank God it has been done"?

Over and over I am asked this question, for this represents a school of thought that insists God *always and only* answers our prayers on the basis of faith.

This school of thought says the way to gain the desired

answers to our prayers is to ask God for what we want, claim the promise that applies, do not doubt for a moment, and begin at once the celebration that the desired result has been obtained.

This reasoning is most often applied when physical healing is sought, but it is also applied to other things— alcohol, drugs, money, and so on.

I remember being in a prayer meeting where a man came forward and laid a package of cigarettes on the altar. The leader laid his hands upon the man's head and prayed like this: "O Lord, You said in Your Word that if we ask anything in prayer, believing, it should be done. Now we ask that this man be delivered from cigarettes, and right now we claim the promise and we thank You and praise You that it has been done!"

He then shook the man's hand and together they praised God that the desired result had been brought to pass. However, in a few days I saw the man back at the same old habit.

Here is another extremely dramatic case of claiming that promise. A couple in their 40s were childless. In their

prayer group their friends gathered about and laid their hands upon the couple (I am not opposed to the laying on of hands; it is scriptural and I have practiced it). Then the friends asked for a baby to be born of the woman, reminded God of His promise, and reminded Him of Sarah and what He did for her. Then they arose and celebrated the pregnancy. The couple marked the date of expectancy on their calendar, bought baby clothing, a bed, and made other preparations.

When sufficient time had passed it became obvious that nothing was going to happen. Their friends were too kind to say it to the disappointed couple, but the only explanation they could offer to one another for God's reluctance was that the couple "didn't have enough faith."

I could go on with some really strange examples of bald men who prayed for hair, on the grounds that "with God nothing is impossible," and others who prayed for new teeth, actually discarding their false teeth in anticipation of the new ones God was going to grow.

Now lest some should think I am poking fun at these dear and earnest people, let me give you another instance with which I am personally knowledgeable. A woman was hospitalized with a most painful disease involving the nerve endings in her skin. She could not bear the slightest touch of sheets, clothing, or hands upon her body. This, of course, rapidly eroded the tolerability level of her nervous system until she was on the verge of complete nervous collapse.

Hospitalized, she had scarcely moved for days. One day the nurse was out of the room, and the phone rang. She had not been able to answer it previously, but this time there was an inner urging that gave her the motivation and strength, and she lifted the phone and answered.

On the other end was a friend who said, "I received the strongest impression possible that God is going to heal you. Now pray this prayer aloud after me."

16

And the friend prayed, "Lord, You said we could ask anything in Your name and You'd grant it. I claim that promise right now, and I praise Your name that *I am in this moment healed!*"

The woman repeated the prayer. The power of God came upon her and she was healed, wonderfully and in a way no one could possibly dispute.

So what does this mean? That the woman who was healed had the proper amount of faith? It doesn't mean that to me, and she will tell you she didn't have "very much" faith when she prayed that prayer.

Here's what all this means to me: it means that *sometimes* the Master Computer-Operator who knows all and sees all with an eternally loving eye says yes to this kind of praying.

The problem is that when this happens people get excited and overzealous, and begin to assume they have finally "found the answer." "It works!" they exult, which really means, "We have found a way to mechanize God and make Him perform. We finally have God boxed in by His own promises, and He can't get out of it!"

Mechanize God? Box in the Holy Spirit? Who is going to put a harness on the wind? Who will regiment a tornado? How can we put power steering on a hurricane?

God is not going to be formularized. You cannot say, "If we do A, B, and C, God will always do D." We may do ABC but sometimes He will do F or M or Z, if it is the *best* thing for those He loves. He will always do what *He* wants to do—you can count on that.

Is it a cop-out to say, "Thy will be done"?

The same school of thought that urges you to ask anything, claim the promise, and celebrate the fact that it has been done, will tell you it is a cop-out to ask and then temper your request with "if it be Thy will."

To some, this is an indication that deep down there lies

17

a doubt that God will perform, that it shows a lack of faith. Therefore, they say, one should never pray and include "if it be Thy will."

Once more, what we believe about prayer reveals the kind of God we believe in. Therefore, if I think it shows a lack of faith to say "if it be Thy will," this will be an indication that I believe in a God who *(a)* responds favorably when the "right" words are said, and unfavorably if the "wrong" words are used, and *(b)* a God who *always* answers prayer on the basis of how much faith the pray-er has.

I do not believe it is a cop-out to use these words. If I do *not* use these words, immediately I have taken away every one of God's options. If He sees and knows a better way, I have insisted my way is the way He must pursue.

God knows the programming of mankind at a glance, not only for the present but also for years and generations to come. For me to tell Him He must answer in *my* way seems insolence unthinkable. Rather than revealing a lack of faith, *to say "if it is Thy will" reveals implicit faith that God's way is ultimately the best.*

Finally, I do not think it a lack of faith to say "If it be Thy will" because of the instruction and example of our Savior. When He gave us the Lord's Prayer as our model, He placed specific emphasis on always praying that our Father's will be done right here, right now, even as it is being done in heaven.

And when under the low-hanging olive branches of Gethsemane our Lord Jesus knelt in agony in prayer, the redemption of mankind was at stake. When all God's hopes and dreams for our salvation hung tremulously upon His decision, Jesus laid it all back on the Father's will.

"If it be possible, remove this cup from Me," He said. In other words, "If there is some other way, if Your perfect will can devise another plan, then do it."

But then, His sweat falling like drops of blood to the ground, He cried, "Nevertheless, not My will but Thine be done." And when He said that, God's will *was* done. So when they led Him down the hill toward the city, there is a sense in which our redemption was already accomplished in the willingness to let God have His way.

Rome crucified His body, Jerusalem crucified His spirit, but He crucified His own will. God, the Master Computer-Operator, the eternal Lover of our souls, was set free to do His perfect will so that once more we might be "at one" with Him.

When I pray should I say "Thee" and "Thou" or "You"?

This seems to bother quite a few people these days, but I am quite sure it doesn't matter one whit to God. It is not the words that the Holy Spirit communicates to God; it is that in the heart which is too deep for words.

But it *is* words that convey impressions of what it means to pray to the ears of listeners who might not know the Lord or who are newborn in the faith. When I was in the pastorate I was once pastor in a college town. College students were present every Sunday. All my life I had prayed in the language of "Thee" and "Thou," but the conviction came to me that the uncommitted young people in my congregation who studied Einstein, Von Braun, relativity, and space mathematics were not likely to be "turned on" by the 450-year-old language of Copernicus.

So I began to address God and to pray in everyday, conversational language, both publicly and privately. It was terribly difficult, for I discovered it was a habit, and I struggled with it for a year before I felt completely comfortable with my new style.

All this is not a plea for *you* to change—not at all; you should be led by the Spirit of God. I only recount this for the benefit of those who frequently pray in public, and they must be led of God and not by me.

19

Praying in the everyday language has helped me bring God from a difficult-to-approach level of loftiness to the level of loving, fatherly nearness.

But the final answer to this question, I believe, is that each person must be led in his own heart, and God will confirm your decision by the degree of comfort you feel in what you are doing—provided, of course, you have consulted Him about it. If you have not asked Him about it, you might simply be comfortable in a familiar habit. But if you have asked Him, that should settle it for you.

How can I keep my mind from wandering?

I have never yet conducted a seminar on prayer but that this question is asked. It obviously springs out of guilt feelings, and this reveals that we believe in a God whose ego is ruffled if we don't give Him our undivided attention.

God is not a dignified old gentleman sitting up in the sky just waiting for someone to offend Him. Besides, He is very patient. The truth of the old hymn "Just as I Am" applies to Christians, too.

However, in spite of this it annoys us to discover that our minds have wandered while we were praying and we have to yank our attention back on course. I am sorry to have to tell you, if you are a young person, that this flaw in our makeup doesn't get any better after one passes 50.

So what to do about it?

A friend helped me with this years ago when he told me that the best preventive for this is to pray aloud. Verbalize the words.

Obviously, mind-wandering is not a problem in praying "flash" prayers; it occurs during our "chunks of time." So just pray aloud. One need not pray so it is audible to a person in the next room; all that is needed is simply to form the lips in a whisper that only we can hear.

This has not completely solved the problem for me, but it has helped immeasurably, and I commend it to you.

Should I always bow my head, close my eyes, and kneel?

Again, habit enters the picture. We are comfortable in our habits, uncomfortable in that which breaks the routine. This is not necessarily a bad thing. We bow and kneel because this is the basic approach we see characters using in the Bible. We have been taught to do it, and it is second nature to us.

We bow our heads not only out of habit but also because we want to recognize that we reverence God. He is much; we are little. The servant bows before the master for the same reason.

God is our Friend, our Companion, the Lover of our souls, our Heavenly Father. He is loving and warm and close, but He is not our fellow-Rotarian or a back-slapping, hail-fellow-well-met. He is *God,* and constant acknowledgment of His Lordship is a "must" for our reborn souls, for their natural tendency is to usurp His creation and take over His throne.

So, reverence is a much-needed quality. We could learn something from the Muslims in this matter. Do you realize there is a reason they wear the "fez," the little brimless hat? In the Far East, the sun is very, very bright. They wear the brimless fez in order that their eyes may be forced downward to avoid the glare of Allah's sun. They do not own hats with brims.

So it is a good thing to bow one's head and close one's eyes. We close our eyes to shut out the world with its distractions, but of course we must finally say our posture has nothing to do with our communication with God. The Holy Spirit does not check to see if we have assumed the prescribed position. Besides, if we are praying while driving

21

down the freeway I wholeheartedly advise against closing the eyes.

The posture we assume is for the sake of our own hearts. This is also true in the matter of kneeling. We can certainly pray standing upright. We do not kneel to get God's attention, but so that He might have ours.

That haughty pride within us that often gives us our spiritual trouble is more likely to be subdued when we are kneeling and bowed down. It is pretty hard to be a big "I am" when one is kneeling before God—possible but not as easy.

If one is in an earthquake or a falling plane, if one is drowning or trapped in a burning building, or suffering a sudden severe heart attack, is God going to say, "Sorry, but you're not kneeling. Sorry, but your head is not bowed and your eyes aren't closed. Therefore you can have no audience with Me"? Ridiculous, of course.

Is it more than coincidence that when dealing with problems of praying we seem always to come back to the true state of the heart? That we always end up depending upon the Holy Spirit to intercede for us with sighs too deep for words—to communicate things to God that we cannot say?

I don't believe it is coincidence. I believe it is "God-incidence."

To whom should I pray? Jesus, the Father, or the Holy Spirit?

It does not matter, for we are not choosing between three Gods. The three are different personal manifestations of God. So we should pray using whatever name makes us feel at ease. Some people could not say, "Dear Holy Spirit" for the life of them, because of various reasons of word associations, and the same is true of "Dear Jesus." Most everybody can say with ease, "Dear God." I do not believe God minds what we call Him.

Personally, I am glad I am able to pray using any of the

three names, but that does not mean I have an advantage over one who cannot.

So whatever difficulty we have in knowing what to call Him merely lies within us and not within God. Therefore, when we pray we should address God in whatever manner is most comfortable for us, always remembering He is more anxious to hear us than to be addressed "properly."

Is it all right to pray for the death of a suffering loved one?

Every time I hear this question it tears me up way down where I live, for I know it has arisen out of the agony of love in a heartrending experience.

Here is a beloved father, perhaps 97 years of age. His life is behind him and he longs for release into the other side, and someone asks me this question. If I say, "Yes, it is all right," then you have the right to ask, "Then just where is cut-off age? At what age do you cease praying for recovery and begin to pray for death? And, besides, is it not a presumptuous thing for a human thus to usurp God's prerogative? Shall He who created life not retain the final right to its cessation? What does love have to say to this?"

I do not know the answer to this one; if I said I did, you would lay this book down and walk away, and you should.

When I was a pastor I prayed for the death of an individual only once. He was bedridden at home, elderly, and ravaged by a terminal disease. He was in what the doctor had only moments before told the family was the final coma.

As I held his hand in prayer before I left, I prayed that God would grant him the mercy of death and release him from the body that was no longer of use to him. I went straight home, and in less than 10 minutes his wife called and told me his soul had gone to the Lord. I bowed my head and thanked God.

Was I right in my prayer? I do not know. I only know

when his wife called I felt a deep sense of peace and thanks-giving.

However, I did not rush right out and begin praying for the death of every "terminally ill" person I met from then on. For one thing, there are too many "terminally ill" people who have been physically healed and are alive and well to-day. I am one of them.

I believe we cannot have a rule about this, but that our hearts should always be sensitive to God's leading from situation to situation, remembering that even if we pray mistakenly the Spirit will communicate to the Father the true intent of our hearts. Further, God will always answer on the basis of what is *best* for the loved one involved, no matter what kind of words we have used (Romans 8:28).

If one of you who are reading these pages has prayed for the death of a loved one, and now you have second thoughts and guilty feelings about it, let me tenderly assure you of a few things: *(a)* You did not pray God into something He didn't want to do. *(b)* If you did it out of love, you did not commit a sin. *(c)* You did not "take the life" of your loved one. *(d)* God is not angry with you. *(e)* You did not deprive your loved one of the opportunity of getting well. *(f)* You did not change God's mind. *(g)* God will not hold it against you.

How should I handle the silences of God?

The most difficult facet of prayer is God's silences. To pray and to see no response is taxing and frustrating to us. If only God would *say* no instead of letting His silence speak for Him! That is when our prayers seem "to go no higher than the ceiling." How often have I heard that, and how often have I experienced it.

Why does God sometimes just leave us dangling in silence when we pray? Obviously, I do not know all the answers to that, but there are *some* answers I can believe and in which my faith is bolstered.

The "hold" button on a telephone helps me here. Sometimes I believe God puts us on "hold." If He is at work in the world and in our circumstances and always working for good for those that love Him, sometimes He himself must wait for the proper tide of circumstances to come about.

Here is a simple illustration. Suppose you live in St. Louis and your son, John, lives in Memphis, and you are praying for his salvation. Suppose also that there is only one other person in the world whom God can use to lead your son to Christ. There is only one other person—Joe—whose personality, views, and ability to relate will appeal to your son strongly enough to influence him in that decision. Joe lives in New York and is planning (unknown to you) to move to Memphis, but not until he has finished his job in New York, which will take a year. Obviously God must put you on "hold" until the circumstances evolve.

Admittedly this is an oversimplification, but it comforts me, for I earnestly believe Romans 8:28 tells infinitely more about our God than we are ever really willing to believe. That in "all things" He is working together for our good, and that the interpersonal relationships involved in all this are only knowable and solvable by the Master Computer-Operator.

God's delays are not *always* denials. There are other reasons God sometimes puts us on hold, or exposes us to His silences. It comforts me deeply to hope and believe that sometimes His silences are really signs of approval. Sometimes He uses them as His very own means to give us a much deeper blessing than He could have otherwise if He rattled off quick answers and easy solutions.

Mrs. Charles E. Cowman, in that classical little devotional book *Streams in the Desert,** illustrates this beautifully in an old familiar story.

A Christian dreamed she saw three others in prayer, and as they knelt the Lord Jesus drew near to them. As He came to the first of the three, He stopped and bent over her. He lingered a long time and spoke to her at quite some length, tenderly and lovingly.

He then came to the next, stopped for only a moment, touched her head, and went on.

He passed by the third woman so abruptly it almost appeared as if He were ignoring her. And the woman in her dream, watching in wonder, said, "How deeply and surely He must love the first one; He approved the second, but the third must have grieved His heart deeply, for He hardly gave her a passing glance!"

But then the Lord of Glory stood beside her and said to her, "O woman, you have wrongly interpreted what you saw. The first praying woman needs all the visible and tangible evidence I can give her of My love and sustaining strength; otherwise she would slip and fall from the narrow way."

He went on, "The second has stronger faith and deeper love, and I can trust her to trust Me however things go and whatever people do.

"But the third woman, whom I seemed not to notice, perhaps even to ignore, and to whom I neither spoke nor touched, has the deepest and most mature faith and love of all. I am training her for the highest and holiest service.

"She knows Me so intimately and trusts Me so utterly that she does not depend upon the outward signs of My voice, nor My touch, nor My spoken approval. She is not dismayed by any circumstances through which she passes. Even when logic and reason seem to dictate rebellion she is not swayed, for she knows beyond doubt that I am working for her here and for eternity to come. She is satisfied to wait for all explanations until later, for she knows whom she has believed!"

So if in the mystery of God's silences we can actually find ourselves praising God for the silence, rejoicing that He has counted us worthy of enduring it, we will not question *why* He has placed us on "hold." For we know that in His own time He will answer the phone.

Now we have tried to meet head-on some of the questions people ask most. Perhaps they will be of help to many, and rebuff others, but upon this by now we all should be able to agree: that human prayer is a mighty weapon in God's arsenal in His warfare against sin and death. It is one of the "big guns" He uses when it is offered. With it He gives flight to the evil one and all his works, and gives answers far beyond what we even ask.

I believe it was writer William Sangster who said, "When we all get to heaven and see what prayer has done, we'll be embarrassed we didn't pray more."

*Compiled by Mrs. Charles Cowman (Grand Rapids: Zondervan Publishing House, 1965), 44. Our thanks to the author, whose address we were unable to locate.

From **You Can Pray as You Ought,** by Arnold Prater. Used by permission.

Chapter 3

Prayer That Helps Your Dreams Come True

by Catherine Marshall

Background Scripture: Matthew 7:7-11

ONE OF THE MOST PROVOCATIVE FACTS I know is that every man-made object, as well as most activity in your life and mine, starts with an idea or a picture in the mind. My mother first taught me this, and at the same time she vividly demonstrated to me the prayer that helps dreams come true.

In my teens I long had the dream of going to college. But this was a depression time and the West Virginia church my father served was suffering financially too. I was accepted at Agnes Scott College in Decatur, Ga., had saved some money from debating prizes, had the promise of a work scholarship —yet we were still several hundred dollars short.

One evening Mother found me lying across my bed,

face-down, sobbing. She sat down beside me. "You and I are going to pray about this," she said quietly. We went into the guest room and knelt beside the old-fashioned, golden oak bed, the one that Mother and Father had bought for their first home. "I know it's right for you to go to college," Mother said. "I believe God planted this dream in you; let's ask Him to tell us how to bring it to reality."

During those quiet moments in the bedroom, confidence and fresh determination flowed in. Mother's faith was contagious. The answer would come. How, we did not know.

I went ahead and made preparations for Agnes Scott. A short time later, Mother received an offer from the Federal

"Dear Lord, connect me with a firm of aggressive professionals with proven track records that will let me pursue rapid career growth with a team of professionals involved in state-of-the-art projects in a solid growth company."

Writer's Project to write the history of the county. Her salary was enough to pay for the major part of my college expenses.

An even more dramatic example of Mother's use of this dreaming prayer involved a young man from "Radical Hill," a run-down section of our West Virginia town. Raymond Thomas, who lived with foster parents, had no idea who his real parents were.

Dressed in working clothes and knee-high clodhoppers, Ray used to come to talk with my mother. He was always clean, but he didn't even own a suit of clothes. On a summer's day he would settle himself on the top step of our vine-shaded front porch talking . . . talking . . . while Mother sat in a wooden rocker shelling peas or stringing beans or darning socks. Mother soon saw his boundless energy and fine mind.

On one particular afternoon there emerged for Ray the same inner longing that I had had—college. Once his dream was out in the open, standing there shimmering, poised in the air, Mother was delighted to see the wistfulness in Ray's brown eyes replaced by kindling hope.

"But how can I manage it?" the boy asked. "I've no money saved. Nor any prospects."

Mother sensed that with Ray, however, the dreaming prayer should involve, more than just college, a completely new approach to life. "Raymond, whatever you need, God has the supply ready for you, provided you're ready to receive it. And ours is still a land of opportunity, Raymond. The sky is the limit! The money will be there for every dream that's right for you, every dream for which you're willing to work."

For a preacher's wife who had little enough herself, this was a doughty philosophy. But Mother believed it and had often proved it so. And these truths took root in Ray.

There came the day when Ray accepted Mother's philosophy so completely that she could lead him in the prayer that releases dreams to make them come true. After having heard her pray it for me, I can easily imagine how it was for Ray. . . . .

"Father, You've given Raymond a fine mind. We believe You want that mind to be developed, that You want Raymond's potential to be used to help You lift and lighten some portion of Your world. Since all the wealth of the world is Yours, please help Raymond find everything he needs for an education.

"And, Father, we also believe You have bigger plans for Raymond. Plant in his mind and heart the vivid pictures, the specific dreams that reflect Your plans for him after college. And oh, give him joy in dreaming—great joy."

With a flat pocketbook but faith in his dream, Raymond Thomas got on a bus and went off to college. How he made it is much too long to chronicle here. It involved Mother's finding a woman to start him off with a loan—writing him encouraging letters—praying. And Ray himself accepting responsibility, developing initiative. In four years he had 12 jobs, budgeting time as well as money: so many hours for classes, study, church work, recreation. It was a proud day for Mother when Ray received his bachelor of science degree, cum laude.

During World War II and afterward I lost touch with Ray, though I knew he had settled in Vienna. Then in the summer of 1958, I wrote Ray that I was coming to Europe.

In Rome I found a letter from him waiting for me. . . .

I have a surprise for you. You will hear from the office of the Reveranda Fabrica di San Pietro whom I've contacted on your behalf. The point is that only with their permission can you see the most wonderful sight in Rome, the excavated street of tombs sixteen centuries old beneath the nave of the High Altar in St. Peter's. I explored every bit of it two years ago. . . .

Then when I checked into the hotel in Florence, the mail clerk handed me another letter from Ray. . . .

31

When you see the high dome of the Duomo, remember that it took Brunelleschi fourteen years to build it. Last winter I climbed to the highest balcony right at the top of the dome and crawled all around it. . . .

By now I was consumed with curiosity about Ray. This man seemed to bear no resemblance to the boy from Radical Hill. Obviously he knew Europe as few Americans do. And the drive and indefatigable zest apparent in his letters intrigued me.

The letters kept coming . . . Venice:

I've written to my friend at the Salviati Glass Works and asked him to send a gondola for you. You must see the master glassblowers at work. . . .

Bad Gastein:

You'll find it rugged. I've skied near there. . . .

Ray met me at the Vienna airport, a bouquet of flowers in hand. "Flowers and music are a part of Vienna," he explained. "Here we always take flowers to our hostess even for a dinner party." Later, over sacher torte and coffee, he began answering my questions. "The fact that I could sit on your front steps and—with no money at all—dream of going to college and achieve it, proved something to me. Very simply, what your mother had said was true—any right dream can be realized. Material resources *are* at the beck and call of the dreamer. And prayer helps you know if it is right and gives you the power to stay with it."

He described his war experience—one of the few survivors of a torpedoed destroyer—and how during convalescence he dreamed of the plan for the rest of his life.

"I wanted to be the kind of world citizen who could serve my country in peacetime, to travel and master several languages, to get a Ph.D. degree."

"It interests me that your dreams were that specific," I interposed.

Ray sipped his coffee, seeming lost in thought as he stared out of the window. "This dreaming process won't work unless we *are* specific. That's because a big part of the power to make the dream come true arises from a mental picture. And you sure do have to have specifics to form a mental picture."

Then Ray went on to sum up how much of his dream had been realized: travel in 60 countries, his Ph.D. in physics from the University of Vienna, which meant mastering German. He also speaks Spanish, passable French, some Italian, Dutch, and Swedish—and a little Russian. He serves his country through a job with the U.S. Atomic Energy Program in Europe.

A story like Ray's reveals the connection between constructive dreaming and prayer. For, in a sense all such dreaming is praying. It is certainly the Creator's will that the desires and talents that He himself has planted in us be realized. God is supremely concerned about the fulfillment of the great person He envisions each of us. He wants us to catch from Him some of His vision for us. After all, this is what prayer is, men cooperating with God in bringing from heaven to earth His wondrously good plans for us.

Sadly, sometimes we fail to catch His vision for us because our capacity to dream has been atrophied by some condition that has given us a poverty complex. My first glimpse of this was in a former college friend who had suffered a poverty-stricken childhood. Dot, as I'll call her, was unable to visualize what she wanted in the vocational field.

Yet she had come to Washington with idealistic ideas about a government job. "I don't want just any job," Dot had explained to me soon after she arrived. "I go along with the idea that God has a plan for my life. Only I haven't yet found it, so how do I pray about this job situation?"

"What job would give you the most joy?" I asked her. "Usually that's a key to what one *should* do."

My friend merely looked puzzled and shook her head.

"Do you ever daydream?" I persisted. "Is there anything you've always longed to do?"

"No—o. Nothing."

The reason that this particular girl could not dream constructively was that during financially difficult years her widowed mother had taught her that those who hope for little or nothing will never suffer disappointment. Actually this had been nothing less than excellent training in poverty expectation. Sadly, I watched my friend fall into a routine government filing job that used but a fraction of her abilities.

I know now that there is healing for such a situation. When we become aware of such damaged areas in the unconscious, we can call on the power of the Holy Spirit. He can walk back with us into the past and drain out all poison, make the rough places smooth, and create a highway for our God to come marching triumphantly into the present with His long-forgotten, oft-delayed plan for our lives.

In fact, there is no limit to what this combination of dreams and prayer can achieve. I have seen amazing results in many areas: like finding the right mate or the right job, or locating the ideal house, or in rearing children, or in building a business.

There are those who are wary of this prayer that helps your dreams come true because they are dubious about praying for material needs such as bread, clothing, a catch of fish, or to put it in modern terms, a parking place for a car. Rightly, they also ask, "Isn't there danger of trying to use God and spiritual principles for selfish ends?"

Each is a valid question that needs to be answered. As for whether God means for us to include material needs in our petitions, certainly Christ was interested in men's bodies as well as their souls. He was concerned about their diseases, their physical hunger. Christianity, almost alone among world religions, acknowledges material things as real and important—real enough that Christ had to die in a real body on a real Cross.

And as for the danger that our dreams may spring from

our selfish human will rather than God's will, there are tests for this. Only when a dream has passed such a series of tests—so that we are certain that our heart's desire is also God's dream *before* we pray—can we pray the dreaming prayer with faith and thus with power.

Let's begin by acknowledging that God's laws are in operation in our universe—whether we recognize them or not. We have to cooperate with these laws, not defy them. For example, ask yourself questions like these:

- Will my dream fulfill the talents, the temperament, and emotional needs that God has planted in my being? This is not easy to answer. It involves knowing oneself, the real person, as few of us do.

- Does my dream involve taking anything or any person belonging to someone else? Would its fulfillment hurt any other human being? If so, you can be fairly sure this particular dream is not God's will for you.

- Am I willing to make all my relationships with other people right? If I hold resentments, grudges, bitterness—no matter how justified—these wrong emotions will cut me off from God, the Source of creativity. Furthermore, no dream can be achieved in a vacuum of human relationships. Even one such wrong relationship can cut the channel of power.

- Do I want this dream with my whole heart? Dreams are not usually brought to fruition in divided personalities; only the whole heart will be willing to do its part toward implementing the dream.

- Am I willing to wait patiently for God's timing?

- Am I dreaming big? The bigger the dream and the more persons it will benefit, the more apt it is to stem from the infinite designs of God.

If your heart's desire can pass a series of tests like this, then you are ready for the final necessary step in the dreaming prayer! Hand your dream over to God, and then leave it in His keeping. There seem to be periods when the dream is like a seed that must be planted in the dark earth and left there to germinate. This is not a time of passiveness on our part. There are things we can and must do—fertilizing, watering, weeding—hard work and self-discipline.

But the growth of that seed, the mysterious and irresistible burgeoning of life in dark and in secret, *that* is God's part of the process. We must not keep digging up our dream, examining and measuring it to see how it is coming along.

Long before we see the fruition of our hopes, in fact the very moment a God-given dream is planted in our hearts, a strange happiness flows into us. I have come to think that at that moment all the resources of the universe are released to help us. Our praying is then at one with the will of God, a channel for the Creator's always joyous, triumphant purposes for us and our world.

Chapter 4

What Are Faith-Sized Requests?

by Rosalind Rinker

Background Scripture: Mark 11:20-24

WHAT IS A FAITH-SIZED REQUEST?

A faith-sized request is first of all a request that is just the right "believing" size for your faith. It is not a request so large that the very size of it makes you wonder if God will answer. It is a request for a particular situation, in which you pray for a special person or thing, and ask only for that which you can *really believe God will do,* in a given time limit. This does not limit what God can do, but it honestly recognizes the size of your faith. And there is every reason to believe that you will be asking for larger things as your faith grows.

Let me illustrate this by a prayer-promise in Mark and also by several true experiences.

Jesus . . . said to them, Have faith in God (constantly). Truly, I tell you whoever says to this mountain, Be lifted up and thrown into the sea! and does not doubt at all in his heart, but believes that what he says will take place, it will be done for him. For this reason I am telling you, whatever you ask for in prayer, believe—trust and be confident—that it is granted to you, and you will [get it] (Mark 11:22-24, Amp.).

The first thing the Lord tells us is to have faith in the One who is able to answer. Then we are told that no matter what mountain stands in our way, if we *ask and believe, it will be moved, it will be done.*

To ask and believe is the opposite of wondering in your heart if you will receive it. That negative picture in your mind of "not receiving" what you asked for is doubt, and doubt will surely keep your prayer from being answered. But God has given us power over our imagination, so that by the positive use of that imagination, we can picture ourselves receiving the answer. This is the way to believe in one's heart, and to believe that what one has asked for, he will receive.

Those are strong, positive words. There is no "if" or "maybe" involved. Why is it, then, that we don't ask for more? Why is it, then, that we seem to get so little when so much is needed?

About the time I began to be aware of honesty and simplicity and brevity in audible prayer, I listened carefully

when others prayed, and also checked myself after I had prayed. I asked myself these questions:

>For what *definite* thing had I prayed?
>
>Did I believe I would get it?
>
>Could I picture myself receiving it?

The tragic answer was that I wasn't asking anything definite, and I wasn't receiving anything definite. I was merely praying platitudes, "Lord, bless my family in America, and bless the Chinese pastors working in Shanghai, and bless ... and bless ... and bless .. ." The words *bless* and *blessing* do get a workout when people pray! But what exactly are we asking for? Are we asking for anything? Are we talking to anyone? Are we expecting an answer from Him?

Two things began to appear in my short, simplified prayers. I saw to it that I thanked Him for something, and I asked Him for something, no matter how small it seemed. It was hard to keep my prayers short at first, but I did it deliberately in order to make myself think specifically, and not just let words flow out without any thought back of them.

And in the asking, I was careful to ask only for that which I believed He could do. If you think it is easy, try it, and keep your mind on being definite. The first thing I knew, I was editing my prayers. I would ask for something, and then quickly ask for forgiveness, because I found I didn't really believe I would get what I was asking for. Then I'd try again and finally I would arrive at one small request (compared to the first one) that I confidently believed God could do and would do in the given situation.

In the past, what I had been doing was like trying to take one giant leap from the bottom of the stairs to the top of the stairs. We *want* to get to the top of the stairs. But it is impossible to get from the bottom to the top of a flight of stairs in one step. Stairs were made to be used, but they were made to be used one step at a time.

The prayer of faith is like that. Climbing the steps is what we mean by a faith-sized request. Take one step at a time. Pray for only what you believe God can do, for a certain person in a definite situation during a given time period.

To illustrate faith-sized requests, I'd like to tell you about a married couple who moved into a new neighborhood. One of the first requests Mary and Jack made was, "Lord, we'd like to get acquainted with our neighbors, and if they don't know You personally as their Savior, we'd like to introduce them to You."

That was a fine request and right in line with what God wanted to do. But it was the description of a goal to be reached, not a step to take. They got down to business then, and took the first step.

"Lord," prayed Jack, "I'd like to meet the fellow living next door in some casual way and begin to get acquainted with him. I'd like to begin today, and I believe You can arrange it for me. Thank You, Lord." Mary agreed with Jack in her prayer, and gave thanks with him.

The morning had scarcely turned to afternoon when the answer came. Their children got into a quarrel over a tricycle with the neighbor's children. Both fathers rushed to the scene. Jack took all the blame for his children, and put out his hand, "I'm Jack M., just moved in, glad to meet you." The first request had been answered. The first step had been taken.

The second step: "Lord, I'd like to know what that man is interested in, so we could become friends." The answer came within two days. He was interested in football.

The third step: "Lord, I need two complimentary football tickets, and could I have them by this weekend, please." The tickets came. The friendship grew.

The fourth step: "Lord, I'd like to invite this new friend to the Bible class I teach a few miles from here. Would You put it into his heart to accept when I ask him to go with me tonight?" He accepted. All the way over as they drove, they talked about football. All the way home they talked about

Jesus Christ and what it meant for Him to become one of us
... God became a Man.

The fifth step: "Lord, Mary and I would like to invite
my friend and his wife to our home some evening this week
and have a little talk and Bible reading together." The
friends came, and they read and talked quietly together.

The sixth step: "Lord, next week when I ask them over
again, will You prepare their hearts, so that they will be
ready to accept You as their Savior? I believe this is the time
to ask for this, and I thank You for all You'll be doing in the
meantime to draw them to Yourself." When the next week
came, the neighbors willingly and gladly accepted Jesus
Christ.

This method works also in matters of guidance about
getting a job, taking a trip, buying or selling a house, getting
married, writing a book, or anything you may think of yourself, small or large.

Here is another illustration. At the Mound Keswick
Conference in Minnesota, I met Rev. Harold De Vries, one of
the speakers. We both attended each other's meetings. My
subjects were conversational prayer and faith-sized requests.

After returning to his church Mr. De Vries spoke to his
people about conversational prayer, and sometime later the
women of the church invited me to speak to them on the
same subject. Two months ago, Mr. De Vries told a friend
something of what was happening among a few groups meeting to pray conversationally.

"Why wouldn't it be a good idea for your people to meet
in small groups and learn to pray like this?" his friend asked.

Mr. De Vries decided he would introduce the subject at
the next Wednesday night prayer meeting. During the day he
asked the Lord to send 150 persons to prayer meeting that
night. Then he remembered "faith-sized requests," and
asked himself if he really believed God could send 150 people.

He changed his prayer. "Lord, I believe You can and will send 100 interested persons to prayer meeting tonight."

There were 100 persons there that night, and they were all interested in forming groups to pray conversationally. By the next Sunday another 50 had signed up, making a total of 150 who are meeting regularly in groups of from 2 to 6 in homes, in offices, in the suburbs, and in the Loop. The needs of the people are being met. Spontaneous prayer is offered for one another, faith-sized requests are being answered, more people are taking part, requests are being covered. There are fewer clichés, less padding, more honesty and simplicity in prayer. Men and women are coming close to God and to each other in the Winnetka Bible church.

The wonderfully exciting thing about faith-sized requests when two or more are praying is that so many times as you pray by subjects, exactly the same request will come to two or more of you at the same time. That is when *faith* rejoices and cries, "It shall be done!" That is the moment when doubt disappears. That is when the whole mountain moves—or sometimes only half of it. But the other half will go, too, if you are willing to wait.

Taken from **Prayer: Conversing with God,** by Rosalind Rinker. Copyright © 1959 by Zondervan Publishing House. Used by permission.

Chapter 5

Prayer in the Valley of Decision

by Lloyd John Ogilvie

Background Scripture: Hebrews 11:8-10, 17-19, 24-27

A FRIEND OF MINE called to arrange a visit over lunch. "I really need to talk with you," he said urgently. "I've got to make a crucial decision about a job offer I have. It could be the most important career decision of my life. My need is for an objective person to listen and tell me how to make a right decision." I told him I'd be happy to listen and share what I'd learned over the years about discovering God's specific will for particular decisions.

When we got together I quickly discovered that the young executive was very serious about wanting to know God's will for the important decision he had to make. He opened the conversation in earnest. "I don't want to make a wrong choice," he said. "But how do I know for sure what is God's will? I really want to take this job, but what if that's just my will and not the Lord's will for me?"

I replied with some questions. "Can you think of any reason the Lord would not want you to make this a yes decision? Will you be asked to do anything contrary to what you believe? Can you continue to put the Lord first in your life if you take this job? Will this opportunity bring you closer to your life goals professionally? Will it give you a chance to witness for your faith? Can you claim the Lord's presence and power as you do your work?"

He could answer all the questions affirmatively. "When do you have to give an answer to the offer?" I asked. He told me he had a few days. Then I suggested an exercise in prayer that has worked for me in making decisions. "It sounds like you really want to take this job. Why not try that on for the days between now and when you must respond. Live with a 'yes' decision. Ask the Lord to create a conviction of right-

44

ness or wrongness. Open yourself in prayer. Yield your mind to Him, surrender your will specifically for this, and ask Him to use everything—circumstances, people you trust, and the Scriptures—to affirm or negate your decision."

A few days later the man called me to tell me that he felt guided to take the job. "I was so concerned," he said. "I thought that because I wanted this, God was probably against it. I couldn't imagine that He would be for me in this!" I reminded him that the Lord was his Friend and wanted what was best for him. He had guided the whole process. Because the man was open to allow the Lord to condition his thoughts, he had been given clear direction. In this case all signals were "go!"

Decisions, decisions. We all face them every day. Some are insignificant; others are crucial for our future. In all of them we want to make guided choices. We long to know and do the Lord's will.

The prophet Joel speaks of the valley of decision. "Multitudes, multitudes in the valley of decision!" (Joel 3:14). Times of making crucial decisions force us into that valley. The alternatives force us to make hard choices.

We Are Not Alone

We are not alone in that valley of decision. The Lord is there with us. His ultimate will for us is that we should know, love, glorify, and serve Him. The Lord also has a personal will for each of us that is His plan for us—unique, particular, and specific.

That does not mean that the Lord's will is a rigid, inflexible set of sealed orders. Rather, the Lord has goals for us, work for us to do, challenges to tackle with His power. Our question is, How do we discover what He wants in each decision?

In every vital decision there is something the Lord does and then something He asks us to do. Let's consider both.

45

What the Lord Does

Would God go to the extents He has to love, forgive, reconcile, and empower us to be His persons, and then leave us without help in making decisions that will shape our destiny?

The Lord doesn't leave us on our own to do that. He loves us so much that prior, during, and after the major decisions of our lives, He takes the responsibility to work in us a clear conviction of what we are to live out.

He Liberates Our Wills

In the consistent communion of prayer, the Lord works to liberate our wills. The will is the implementer of thought and desire. Thus the Lord's task in us is to clarify His will. The wonder of it all is that He can and will enable us to desire what He desires for us. He gives us an eager mind that wants to discover His strategy for our lives. Our thoughts are purified by prolonged and repeated times of prayer.

So often we feel we are solely responsible for our decisions. When a big one comes along we think that we should check in with the Lord to get help. Then soon we forget our need of His continuing guidance and live on our own ability. That's to miss the hourly and daily direction He offers.

The Lord knows the future. He foresees the decisions that are ahead of us. Long before the decision must be made, He begins His preparation in us. He uses everything in and around us to condition our thoughts and will in anticipation. The habitual communion of prayer and Bible study gives us the convictions, ideas, and values that will affect our understanding at the time of the decision. Repeated relinquishment of our will makes us ready and receptive.

The question I'm asked most often is, How can I know the will of God? My answer is not to give people a set of rules to finding God's will but to explain His promise to work in us constantly so that we are ready for the choices of life. That

46

leads to the discipline of prayer, not just for crises, but in daily times of listening and constant communion through the day. That's often more than people bargain for who raise the question about how to know God's will.

Over the years, I have discovered that the Lord does not distribute cheap grace and guidance. He created us for a consistent companionship and redeemed us to live in close oneness with Him. Those who rush to Him only when a decision demands His help are often made to wait. He uses the time of indecision to draw us closer to Him and establish a profound relationship that will prepare us for decisions in the future.

I have a friend who calls her doctor only when she has an illness. She talks to him on the phone and wants a prescription of some miracle drug for whatever malady she has. Consistently, she has resisted general checkups and the doctor's desire to help her with an overall plan of diet, exercise, and health care, which would avert her repeated illnesses. Recently he refused to give quickie remedies on the phone and told her she must submit to his comprehensive program of care for her long-range well-being. That would necessitate more than a phone call in crises. The doctor cared too much for this woman's health to continue as a telephone prescription service.

How much more the Lord wants to maximize our spiritual lives. He is up to momentous things with us. In His master plan for the kingdom in our time, He has plans for each of us that fit into His overall will. The people around us, the churches of which we are a part, the places we work, and the communities in which we live are dependent on our seeking the Lord's will consistently so that His maximum in every area can be accomplished. When we are out of touch with Him, we make wrong choices, develop unguided programs, and head in directions that are less than He envisions for us. We and others are cheated.

Hebrews 13:20-21 sounds a trumpet call for those who seek God's will. "May the God of peace, who through the blood of the eternal covenant brought back from the dead our Lord Jesus, the great Shepherd of the sheep, equip you with everything good for doing his will, and may he work in us what is pleasing to him, through Jesus Christ, to whom be glory for ever and ever."

The Lord has called us to be His people and will not let us go. As He took responsibility for our redemption, He assumes the initiative role in "making us complete." The word for "complete" in this stirring passage means "to equip." The Lord equips us to do His will. As indwelling Lord living in us He gives us whatever we need to know and do His will. He wants us to do what is well pleasing in His sight. But He does not leave that for us to flounder about until we happen on it. He readily responds to our willingness and makes His will known for each situation, choice, and decision.

What Is Our Part?

Now, in response to these awesome promises we must consider what our part is in discovering and doing the Lord's will in our decisions. There are three gifts we have to give: An open mind, a responsive will, and a faithful obedience.

An Open Mind

Prayer is the time in which what the Lord has been "working in us" is worked out in clarified thought. *An open mind is attentive.* What He has been developing in our thoughts about His specific guidance is crystallized. When we wait quietly in His presence, the Lord will reform our thinking around His plans for us. Bible commentator William Barclay said, "Here is something to ponder. We are so apt to think that prayer is asking God for what we want, whereas true prayer is asking God for what He wants. Prayer is not only talking to God, even more it is listening to Him."[1]

I find it helpful to say to the Lord, "I consciously yield my capacity to think, which You gave me to guide me in thinking Your thoughts." That keeps me from falsely using prayer as a means of persuading God to do what I want. True prayer is intelligent, purposeful conversation with God in which our thinking is reoriented and redirected.

My good friend Paul Rees put it this way, "If we are willing to take hours on end to learn to play the piano, or operate a computer, or fly an airplane, it is sheer nonsense for us to imagine that we can learn the high art of getting guidance through communion with the Lord without being willing to set time aside for it. It is no accident that the Bible speaks of prayer as a form of waiting on God."[2] But it is not waiting for God to hear, but waiting until our minds are quiet and receptive enough to receive what He has been waiting to communicate. Our task is to offer the Lord an open mind.

A Responsive Will

A responsive will is closely intertwined with an open mind. The will can be either a sentinel guarding the door of a closed mind or a ready servant to carry out what the Lord articulates in our thoughts. The persistent prayer, "Lord make me willing to hear and desire what You want," is the key. Since He motivates the longing to pray that prayer, He is ready to answer it.

A completely surrendered will opens the floodgate for the Lord to work in our minds "to will and do His good pleasure." We will not know His will or desire to do it until we ask for the miraculous healing of our wills. We will remain willful and stubborn until He sets us free.

A Faithful Obedience

Faithful obedience is the direct result of that freedom. The Lord progressively reveals His will to those who act on what He guides. Often we find it difficult to desire His will in a crucial decision because we have resisted acting on what He has clearly guided in other areas of our relationships and responsibilities. We get prepared for life's big decisions by following through with obedience in what we know He has asked us to do in daily faithfulness to Him. We need to ask Him, "Lord, is there any area where I have been unwilling? Give me courage to follow orders today so that You can trust me with guidance in the future." We do not know what demanding decisions are ahead. Preparation for them begins now.

I have found that journaling is a helpful discipline. Each day as a part of prayer and Bible study I try to log the insights I have received and steps of obedience I feel the Lord guides. It provides a good inventory when I return to my quiet time the next day. I can check off things that have been done and be reminded of unfinished orders. I also list specific petitions for the Lord's will under each day's entry. It is a great source of gratitude and praise to go back over a year's record of requests for guidance and realize how the Lord answered. I am filled with thanksgiving for what He has done and refortified for the future.

Abraham Lincoln puts an exclamation point on what I've tried to communicate about the Lord's guidance in our decisions. During the dark days of the Civil War, the Lord gave him direction and strength. Over 120 years ago, the same year he reestablished a National Day of Prayer, Lincoln said, "I have been driven many times to my knees by the overwhelming conviction that I had nowhere else to go; my own wisdom and that of all around me seemed insufficient for the day."

And then, explaining the Lord's answers, the president said, "I have had so many evidences of His direction, so many instances of times when I have been controlled by some other power than my own will, that I cannot doubt that this power comes from God. I frequently see my way clear to a decision when I am conscious that I have not sufficient facts on which to found it. I am satisfied that, when the Almighty wants me to do, or not to do a particular thing, He finds a way of letting me know. I talk to God, and when I do, my mind seems relieved and a way is suggested."

1. William Barclay, *Daily Study Bible, 1 John* (Philadelphia: Westminster Press, 1959).

2. Paul Rees, from a sermon.

Chapter 6

Bearing One Another's Burdens

by Madalene Harris

Background Scripture: Luke 22:31-32; 1 Timothy 2:1-8

WHAT'S A POOR MOTHER to do with a houseful of quarrelsome, headstrong children? Four *is* a houseful, isn't it? That was exactly my predicament for 10 years when my husband traveled and left me alone to manage this unmanageable situation. It was during those years that I stumbled upon the most powerful principle of my life.

Being isolated in a beautiful mountain setting, while inspiring, only compounded my bewilderment, which often grew to desperation. At first I tried to postpone major decisions and severe disciplinary action until my husband returned. But problems merely intensified, and soon I discovered two indisputable facts: neither discipline nor decisions can be delayed where young children are concerned, and settling disputes was the last thing my husband welcomed during his few days home.

When the full impact of this discovery penetrated my battle-fatigued brain, I felt as forlorn as a newborn puppy lost in a rainstorm. I didn't know which way to turn. Until, that is, I entered the charmed circle of God's sure-fire remedy for impossible situations.

Every morning after the children were safely deposited on the school bus, I grabbed my Phillips New Testament and

my well-worn devotional book, *Streams in the Desert.* Running alongside the tumbling stream that flowed through our yard, I jogged the mile or so to a secluded spot and there I poured out my heart to the Lord. Thus began my practice of daily earnest prayer for my children.

Amazing things happened. Attitudes changed; the noise level at our house decreased; my nerves grew steadier. I discovered that the children's temperaments (and my own) improved in direct proportion to my faithful prayer vigil on their behalf.

As time progressed and I witnessed our household gradually changing, I wondered whether this same principle would apply to other people. Slowly my faith muscles began to flex and grow strong with consistent exercise, and I slipped into my Bible a thin pad on which I scribbled names as the Lord directed. My prayer life, which had begun out of desperation, was being swept along by the spontaneous winds of daily anticipation of God at work.

One day while sitting on a rock beside our creek and reflecting upon clear instances of God intervening in circumstances in answer to prayer, a thought slowly dawned upon me: *What I'm doing is intercession.* When I returned home, I checked the precise meaning of the word in my dictionary. Three sentences confirmed my suspicions. Interceding included pleading or petitioning on behalf of one in difficulty or trouble; mediating or attempting to reconcile differences; praying to God on behalf of another or others.

Previous Programming

Suddenly I remembered a long-forgotten picture stored away in the recesses of my mind. While in college I had been deeply impressed by an artist's concept of intercession.

The picture displayed a powerful hand extending down from the clouds into a circle representing the world. Familiar shapes of continents clearly identified the sphere. A smaller hand and forearm covered with slimy mud, which represented the decadent nature of the world, reached up and grasped the larger hand. That was all. A single-word caption spoke volumes: *intercession.*

As I mentally recaptured the illustration and the impact it had made upon my spirit, I also remembered my fervent prayer. "Lord, that's what I want to be—an intercessor."

With the pressures of the daily grind, however, I had forgotten my prayer. But God hadn't and now He was showing me that I could be so deeply immersed in this exciting adventure that my heart seemed to be almost spontaneously flowing to the heart of God.

Developing Perspective

Having finally understood the nature of my pursuit, it was time to determine how deeply I intended to commit myself. I could not pray for everyone. That became obvious, but how much time I would spend, how many people I would include, and upon what basis I would make my requests became serious considerations. A strong sense of destiny gripped me as I sought answers.

The most important decisions involved firmly establishing time and place. In the summertime I had to get away from the house, children, and telephone. My secret hideaway down by the creek served well. In winter when the children were gone, my bedroom became my altar. (I never hesitated to take my phone off the hook.)

Early in the day, before crises developed, was best for me and I found that the amount of time spent varied. Some days I dared leave my busy household for only 15 minutes. Other times a whole hour proved insufficient. I have learned to stay before the Lord until He releases me.

About that time I learned of a daily prayer diary published by Campus Crusade's Great Commission Prayer Crusade. When I received mine, a huge problem of mental organization resolved itself. The notebook was divided into separate categories: personal requests for which I would pray every day; requests for which I would pray once a week (a list for Mondays, a list for Tuesdays, and so forth); and a section for temporary requests. Maintaining separate lists of prayer objects multiplied my effectiveness. (A revised version of this diary is now called *Vonette Bright's Prayer and Praise Diary*, published by Here's Life Publishers.)

For Whom Do I Pray?

My final dilemma, how to select names for my prayer notebook pages, became no huge consideration. To state it simply, I just knew whom God wanted me to include. No big deal. My heart became—and still becomes—strangely burdened. Or, to phrase it in scriptural terminology, my heart burns within me, and I sense divine direction.

Some of the entries on my pages include the following:

Monday—My nation; the president, his decisions, his health, his wife, his spiritual needs; critical issues publicized in the media; all Christians in political office; revival in our country.

Tuesday—My church: all staff members, their families; my special friends; critical needs; issues; problems.

Wednesday—Ministries: the Christian radio programs I listen to; worldwide television outreaches; other ministries that have touched my life.

Thursday—Personal friends in ministry and elsewhere.

Friday—Foreign countries my husband and I have visited and the gospel ministries there: Japan, Korea, Israel, Mexico.

Saturday—Unbelieving relatives and friends.

Sunday—My husband's and my personal ministry needs.

Daily personal—My children, their families, all requests concerning our personal lives. (I use photographs for visualization. Opposite this page I have pasted a small picture of our entire family. Above it I printed "You have not because you ask not. Ask and you shall receive." Below it are the words, "Is anything too hard for God?")

Do I ever remove a name or cause? Only when I sense an inward release. Often when I've had no contact with a person for an extended period, I decide to delete the entry. Sometimes I can. Sometimes God says, "No, keep on praying."

Powerful Promises

"What keeps you faithful?" people often ask. "Don't you ever get burned out and just let it slide?"

Although many factors contribute toward my persistence, overriding them all is the persuasive knowledge that a unique blessing is promised in relation to this ministry.

Consider, for example, these Scripture passages: Jesus said, "I will do whatever you ask in my name, so that the Son may bring glory to the Father. You may ask me for anything . . . and I will do it" (John 14:13-14). I have yet to untangle the theological knots in the terms *whatever* and *anything.* I may never accomplish it. But that doesn't keep me from believing that God means exactly what He says and from acting upon it. Further, note Mark 9:23: "Everything is possible for him who believes." Or James 5:16: "Pray for each other so that you may be healed. The prayer of a righteous man [woman] is powerful and effective."

These are but three of hundreds of prayer promises sprinkled throughout the Bible. How can I question the validity of God's Word? In fact, when I consider the scores of times Jesus himself told us our prayers would be answered, I marvel that I don't spend all of my time interceding.

Jesus is, in fact, an interceder's prime example. He said to Peter, "Satan has asked to sift you as wheat. But I have prayed for you, Simon, that your faith may not fail" (Luke 22:31-32). And doesn't Hebrews 7:25 say that "He always lives to intercede for them [us]"?

When I review the emphasis God's Word places upon

the prayer of intercession, I am compelled to cry with Samuel, "Far be it from me that I should sin against the Lord by failing to pray for you" (1 Samuel 12:23).

Is Desire Necessary?

Does praying always fit into my schedule?

No. My life is no different from yours. To live in the 20th century is to encounter pressures and distractions that squeeze the life from spiritual desire and steal time from our schedules.

Often I compare the exercise of prayer to my daily running regimen. I must confess that I seldom feel like lacing up my Nikes and heading outside. And all I think about during the first 10 minutes is quitting. Sometimes that's all I think about during the entire routine. But I do it anyway, and, no matter how I feel about jogging at the moment, I still reap the wonderful benefits.

So it is with prayer. Hudson Taylor, whose life has been a shining inspiration to me, once said, "Sometimes when I pray, my heart feels like wood, but often the choicest answers come from those prayers." So I tell myself that it really doesn't matter how I feel. Frankly, God doesn't trouble himself with my feelings about His commandments. His chief concern is that I obey.

Fringe Benefits

Is it all give and no take? What does the intercessor gain from daily sacrifice of valuable time and the grueling discipline often demanded? Anything except the assurance of obeying God?

Obedience is a reward in itself, but there are other benefits: the privilege of participating in a powerful, God-honoring ministry without leaving home is high compensation. Christians everywhere are searching for a meaningful method of reaching people for Christ. Here is one that can be found, without a search. Instead of being mere spectators of God's great drama, we can become strategically involved in the lives of people all around the world.

Another fulfilling aspect of this private ministry is my children's faith. As they have seen results, they have subconsciously learned what no amount of lecturing could have taught them: "God always answers prayer; therefore it pays to pray." Especially my younger son, David, made known his dependence on God's answers to my prayers. Throughout his college and seminary years, our long-distance calls included conversations such as, "Mother, I have three exams this week. Would you please write down the days and times so you can pray while I'm taking them?"

On the humorous side, all of my children (now grown) know that most weekday mornings while I am writing, I take my telephone off the hook. Three of them live locally; only David lives out of town.

One morning while writing my second book, I felt a strong urge to walk over and put the receiver back on its cradle. Resisting, I thought, That's foolish. My writing is going too well to be interrupted. So I proceeded, but soon the urgent impulse recurred. Sighing, I arose and replaced the phone, and before I returned to my desk, the phone rang.

"Mother, I'm so glad you put your phone back," David began. "I need to talk to you so badly, and I've been trying all morning to get through. Finally I gave up and said to the Lord, 'Please tell my mom to put her phone on the hook.'"

Now, whenever my other children complain about not being able to reach me in the morning, I simply smile and say, "You aren't using the right technique. Try David's."

Tips for Intercessors

Here are some pointers to help you get started on your prayer journey.

1. We learn by doing—not reading about it.

2. Quieting inner restlessness will be your greatest challenge. The flesh loves to be active. Be persistent. (Keep

59

a pad and pen handy to jot down darting thoughts concerning important tasks to be done during the day. Then put them out of your mind.)

3. Set aside a specific time and place and be as prompt with this appointment as with any other. This is not "prayer on the run."

4. Keep a prayer diary.

5. Be specific with your requests. Generalization dulls the imagination and creates loss of incentive.

6. Visualize. Make mental pictures of the situations or people for which you are praying. See them as God sees them.

7. Operate on a "revelation" basis. Let God show you for whom to pray, how long, and when to stop.

8. Pray blessings upon your enemies. Forgive everyone so your prayers will not be hindered.

9. Don't forget our country's leaders. "I urge . . . that . . . intercession and thanksgiving be made for everyone—for kings and all those in authority" (1 Timothy 2:1-2).

10. Never give up. Never, never, never. "Pray without ceasing."

Personal Postscripts

The children are gone. The house is quiet. New pressures have replaced those that once drove me to the secret place. Since the clamor of immediate demands has silenced, do I slacken my daily vigil on behalf of my children and others?

This may sound strange, but the burden of intercession weighs more heavily than ever. Although three of my four are involved in direct Christian ministry, I am haunted by the realization that I could be the only person in the world praying for them. Certainly I hope I'm wrong. Just in case I am not, however, I keep my daily appointment at the throne of grace.

Now that my children are physically removed from me,

I pray, "Lord, help me to know their deepest needs so I can effectively intercede for them." And it's amazing how God clues me in. One of my young grandchildren might slip, "Grandma, we don't have any money." Or a chance remark might register deeply in my mind and provide the insight I need. If one of them seems to be heading in a wrong direction, I never say anything. I simply take my observations to a higher Source and ask Him to solve the problem.

Sidlow Baxter succinctly expressed my thoughts when he said, "Men may spurn our appeals, reject our message, oppose our arguments, despise our persons—but they are helpless against our prayers."

With such a weapon just a breath away, how can I excuse negligence or procrastination? Won't God hold me accountable for knowing to do good and refusing? If I, by sacrificing a small portion of my day, can lift the load of my fellow believers, brighten their spirits, and encourage their hearts, how can I afford to withhold this "cup of cold water" that my Father asks me to offer?

Chapter 7

How to Pray for Healing

by Stan Meek

Background Scripture: John 9:1-7; 2 Corinthians 12:7-10; James 5:13-16

I WONDER how serious many of our petitions for healing really are. Are they prayers we pray only casually, or maybe even "frantically" while we more seriously seek help from other sources? Or are they prayers prayed out of a well-defined Bible belief about divine healing?

The Bible has a lot to say about the healing of disease. Prayer and healing are linked in both the Word of God and the practices of the Early Church. To the leper who came to Jesus, saying, "Lord, if you are willing, you can make me clean," Jesus simply said, "I am willing. . . . Be clean!" and "Immediately he was cured of his leprosy" (Matthew 8:2-3).

Matthew says Jesus "went throughout Galilee teaching in their synagogues, preaching the good news of the kingdom, and healing every disease and sickness among the people" (4:23). Jesus gave to the "Twelve" and to the "Seventy" authority not only to preach but also to *heal*. They were active in this ministry even after the Ascension and during the developing years of the Early Church.

Some Bible scholars view healings and other miraculous interventions as primarily dispensational (temporary power granted by God, to help get the Early Church started). But Christian literature and testimony reveal that miraculous healings and signs are still taking place today and that this was not just limited to the founding days of the Church.

There is a tablet in the back of a church in Lucknow, India, that reads, "Near this spot Stanley Jones knelt a physically broken man and arose a physically well man." E. Stanley Jones, by his own testimony, was at his "rope's end" in his missionary work. But he went on from his healing in

"Cheer up, Reverend, we'll have you up and back on your knees again in no time."

1917 to give 54 more years of fruitful evangelism to the world. He called it an "unconditional" healing—direct, radical, and instantaneous.

This is just one of countless thousands of well-documented modern examples of divine healing. Today's Christian magazines are filled with first-person case histories of God's supernatural help, healing, and intervention.

Dr. William Sadler, an eminent physician, has declared that "in neglecting prayer for healing, we are neglecting the greatest single power in the healing of disease." Another prominent surgeon, speaking at a breakfast gathering for clergymen in Dodge City, Kans., said, "The truth is, as doctors, we don't have nearly as many answers for man's needs this side of death as people think we do. And we have none for the other side."

His admission does not diminish our respect for the medical field and its enormous contribution toward health care. We do not have to neglect the blessings of medical science to enjoy the advantages of praying for healing.

Could it be, though, that too often, people do not really know the Bible prescription for sickness? Is it possible that many are afraid of getting serious about praying for healing? Afraid of being considered "radical"? Afraid of what people will say if they are *not* healed?

The fact that some have abused the privilege of praying for healing by commercializing it, or by treating it like a "fetish," does not in the least diminish its power or value. What legitimate thing has not been abused?

Jeremiah prayed, "Heal me, O Lord, and I will be healed; save me and I will be saved, for you are the one I praise" (17:14). This biblical prayer for healing teaches us we ought to pray for healing. It points us to the true source of all healing. It demonstrates simple faith. It connects healing and salvation, as did James in the New Testament. And it relates *praise* to prayer and healing. Jeremiah's prayer is a worthy model.

How Important Is the Asking?

There are many things we don't receive from God simply because *we do not ask.* Many people are not healed from their sicknesses because they have either ignored God's healing power, or they have treated it as a second-rate possibility.

Frank Bateman Stanger, a Christian writer, reminds us, though, that prayer is so related to healing that "it is instinctive for persons of faith to seek healing through prayer." This was beautifully illustrated for me just recently.

I had the privilege of watching a saint die. He had lived by faith and by the Scriptures. Even though he was 84 years old and had terminal cancer of the liver, he instinctively turned to the Lord for healing. He asked that I anoint him for healing, as the Bible instructs.

He said, "Pastor, I'm not clinging to life. In fact, when it comes to the end, I don't want them to use any life-support systems; I don't want to be kept here. But I believe we ought to do what the Bible says." He was talking about James 5:14, "Is any one of you sick? He should call the elders of the church to pray over him and anoint him with oil in the name of the Lord."

Not only must we ask seriously but we must ask in faith as well. It is obvious that Jeremiah had faith in God for healing. He said simply, "Heal me, O Lord, and I will be healed." That is faith.

Perhaps the single most important factor in receiving healing is to ask in simple faith. The Bible says, "And without faith it is impossible to please God, because anyone who comes to him must believe that he exists and that he rewards those who earnestly seek him" (Hebrews 11:6).

James says, "The prayer offered in faith will make the sick person well; the Lord will raise him up" (5:15). That is a promise as sure as any promise in the Word of God. Believe it for *your* sickness. It is a simple promise; it requires only simple faith.

Are Salvation and Healing Related?

It is important that salvation and healing are related in the Bible. In fact, *health* and *salvation* are the same word in Scripture. They are connected here in Jeremiah's prayer. They are connected in the instructions of James regarding the sick, and Jesus certainly related them (Mark 2:1-12).

A proper understanding of this fact will save us from erroneous beliefs and practices about divine healing.

The connection between health and salvation helps us understand that God is more interested in our holiness than in our physical healing. This is a distinction that is hard to keep clear in a "fallen world" that is preoccupied with immediate comforts. The connection between health and holiness, no doubt, also explains some of the delays and denials in answer to our prayers.

The late Bible scholar C. S. Lewis called pain "God's intolerable compliment." God's very mercy and love for me may prevent His dashing to my every discomfort with instant deliverance. He wants my total wholeness and healing—spiritually as well as physically.

Sheldon Vanauken's beautiful love story, *A Severe Mercy,* is an account of how God had to break through the "shining barrier" of his and his wife's tightly insulated love. Sheldon was led to see, through the letters of his friend, C. S. Lewis, how his wife's death was simply "a severe mercy" from God intended to bring him into a relationship with God—a relationship he never seemed to have room for because of his love for his wife.

Glaphré Gilliland, who has had a powerful effect on our times with her prayer ministry, said of her own efforts to cope with disease, "I was wanting God to change my circumstances. God was wanting to change me." God allows some sickness and suffering in this world in order to bring about a more perfect and permanent healing for eternity.

What if Healing Doesn't Come?

This connection between holiness and healing will also protect us from unbalanced scriptural views of healing. A balanced perspective on the whole of Scripture as well as human experience must acknowledge not only the possibility of great cure but also the possibility of continued suffering and death—even when the sincere prayer of faith is offered.

E. Stanley Jones was "unconditionally" healed at one time in his life. But nevertheless, much later, he had a stroke. Out of this "handicap" he was to write his final and beautiful book, *The Divine Yes,* in which he describes God's keeping grace in the midst of sickness. God does not always heal unconditionally.

And what about Joni Eareckson Tada? Why has a wonderful Christian woman like her never been healed? Some would no doubt say she just hasn't "named it and claimed it." Others would imply that her faith must not be strong enough. And perhaps some "absolutists" would even say there's sin in her life.

The words of Jesus, "Neither this man nor his parents sinned" (John 9:3), teach us not to accuse every sick person of sin. Who would deny, for example, the powerful impact that Joni's fully redeemed life has had through her paralytic, not yet fully redeemed body? And who is to know whether her life would have been lived to glorify God had she been instantly delivered from her handicap?

While Christ's atonement has provided for healing and deliverance, God will remain sovereign. He will not be manipulated even within the triumphs of the atonement. Neither will He be confined to our time scheme.

Again, Glaphré writes pointedly about this: "A dangerous exchange—this switching roles with God. This belief that God must act on *our* conclusions of what is best and needed. This requiring God to fulfill *our* desires *our* way." She continues, "What happens when God doesn't jump through the hoop we hold up? Especially when the hoop-jumping and errand-hopping is the only kind of help we want from God."

There do not seem to be any simple and final answers to the question of suffering and healing in this life. Therefore, don't be intimidated by some popular "priest" of the health-wealth-and-prosperity cult who claims to "understand it all"—that "priest" who tells you if you aren't healed, or if you aren't driving Cadillacs instead of Chevys, you simply don't have enough faith, or there's sin in your life.

Admittedly, there are some divine promises people are not taking seriously. But there are also some promises being promoted that just don't square with the whole of Scripture or with human experience. God is too great, humanity is too deep, and individualism is too important for God's methods of dealing with people or their diseases to become stereo-typed. God will not heal the disease of everyone who, in faith, asks for healing.

Writer Geoffrey King says that God allows some suffering in this world to gender sincere and true sympathy. He says, "If we could cure every sickness, the heart of this world would become as hard as stone."

So, we must avoid the error of believing that God wills the immediate cure of every sickness. At the same time, we must avoid accepting every sickness as "God's will," or something we must endure.

And while sickness does not necessarily imply sin in our life, every sickness ought to get our attention and cause us to ask, "Is God trying to say anything to me in this?" Perhaps God is not trying to say anything, and the sickness is just a consequence of our fallen world. But God has been known to occasionally use illness to get our attention and teach us something.

We need to be serious about seeking healing from *every* disease. As Don Bubna, pastor of the Alliance church in Salem, Oreg., says, "The ultimate healing will be our resurrection . . . but between now and then we have the privilege of asking God to intervene."

Because of Calvary, we have that privilege. Because of the Resurrection, we have the gift and power of faith, and we can rest the results in the unquestioned goodness of the Conqueror of death.

Charles Farr, pastor of the Church of the Epiphany in Denver, says, "God wants us to be healed even if it means dying well." The 84-year-old saint I mentioned was healed in that manner. He died as he lived. I have never seen a Christian die so nobly. And after all, isn't that what we, His children, want to do—to live and to die for the praise of His glory?

Chapter 8

The Question of Unanswered Prayer

by Lloyd John Ogilvie

Background Scripture: Job 23:2-7; 42:2-5

SOME TIME AGO I gave a series of messages on prayer to my congregation in Hollywood. One Sunday morning, as I greeted the people after one of these messages, a woman pressed a carefully folded note into the palm of my hand. She held my hand firmly as I looked into her eyes long enough to know that whatever was written on the note was urgent and the expression of an honest need. I thanked her for it and assured her that as soon as I had finished with the greeting I would read it and respond.

When I reached my study and had a few leisure moments to unfold the note, this is what I read: "Lloyd, I have appreciated all the positive things you have said about how to pray with power, but I must be very honest. This series on prayer has made me feel very lonely, even a bit angry at times. I look around me as you tell all the glorious things that happen when we pray and see everyone nodding in agreement and affirmation. Doesn't anyone feel the way I do about those times when prayer is unanswered? Here's my problem. For months now I've had the feeling that God neither heard nor responded to my prayers. I have gone from feelings of guilt that something must be wrong with me, to doubt about whether God cares. I just had to tell someone— to ask the lurking question—why are some prayers unanswered?"

Ever feel that way? Have you ever known an excruciating dry spell in your prayers when there seemed to be no answer to your prayers? Of course, we all have. Deep down inside of all of us are questions about why prayers sometimes seem like an endless monologue.

There are some who have never had what they would call a definite answer to prayer. Others have known the ecstasy of sweet communion with the Lord in prayer and have also found that for some strange reason, prayer has suddenly become sterile and unrewarding. Still others are like this woman. You have prayed, waited, wondered, and become weary. And then there are others of us who wrestle with the bold promises of the Bible about prayer and are frustrated by the disparity of what is offered and what we seem to experience in our prayers. We follow Jesus' admonition to ask, seek, knock. We read that all we are to do is make our requests known and they will be granted. "If you ask anything in My name, I will do it" (John 14:14, NKJV), He promises with assurance. Why then the problem of unanswered prayer?

The Lord loves us very much. He wants us to express how we are feeling about those times when our prayers seem not to be answered. The question from the deeps of our souls will be answered from the depth of His love. But while we are questioning Him, He may have some very crucial questions to ask us.

That's what happened to Job. The story of Job's suffering is a classic study of the problem of unanswered prayer. Job was a prosperous man who lost everything—his wealth, children, cattle. Along with these, he also almost lost his faith in the righteous justice of God. His friends tried to convince him that he must have sinned in some way to have brought this punishment from God. They espoused the belief held at that time that suffering was the recompense of God for sin. Job protested his innocence. But most acutely he felt the absence of God when he cried out for vindication.

72

He tried to maintain his belief in the righteousness of God and his conviction that, if he could only reach Him, he could question the Almighty about the injustice he was enduring, and why He would allow it. Most of all, Job wanted the Lord's presence and assurance.

Finally, after a prolonged time of what seemed to be no answer from God to his prayer, Job borders on bitterness.

The time when we wonder about unanswered prayer is also God's time to question us. That's what He did to Job. The Lord faces Job with his arrogant pride, which has questioned the purpose, power, and providence of the Creator and Sustainer of the universe.

Listen to some of the questions the Lord asked Job. "Where were you when I laid the foundations of the earth? Tell Me, if you have understanding. Who determined its measurements? Surely you know! Or who stretched the line upon it? To what were its foundations fastened? Or who laid its cornerstone, when the morning stars sang together, and all the sons of God shouted for joy?" (Job 38:4-7, NKJV). Throughout the rest of chapters 38—40 the Lord mounts confrontive questions that expose Job's arrogant questioning of the Almighty. Who controls the sea? Who commands the morning and the cycle of day and night? Who sets the length of a person's life? All the questions of God reach a crescendo with the ultimate demand to one who demanded that He be accountable: "Shall the one who contends with the Almighty correct Him? He who rebukes God, let him answer it" (Job 40:2, NKJV).

At last, in humble submission, Job surrendered his demand that the Lord justify himself to him. In the last chapter of the Book of Job, we witness how the Lord dealt with the sufferer. God answered Job's prayers not with any self-justifying explanation but with His presence. Then Job is able to pray, "I know that You can do everything, and that no purpose of Yours can be withheld from You. You asked, 'Who is this who hides counsel without knowledge?' Therefore I have uttered what I did not understand, things too wonderful for me, which I did not know. Listen, please, and let me speak; You said, 'I will question you, and you shall answer Me.' I have heard of You by the hearing of the ear, but now my eye sees You" (Job 42:2-5, NKJV).

The question of unanswered prayer is not really our question at all, but the Lord's. What He asked Job, He asks us. "Who is this who hides counsel without knowledge?" Or put another way, "Who is this who withholds answers to our prayers without purpose?" The question forces us to think much more humbly about our audacious questioning of God. But the question also prompts the Lord's penetrating questions, not unlike the ones given to Job but with greater impact. The Lord reviews for us not only His creation but also His redemptive acts in Jesus Christ. It is at the foot of the Cross, beside an Empty Tomb, in a Pentecost Upper Room, that He questions us about His readiness to answer prayer. "What more need I do?" And our response is, "Nothing, Lord, just give us Your presence and all our questions will melt away!"

Job has taught us three crucial things about our dilemma with unanswered prayer.

All Prayers Are Answered

The first is that *all prayers are answered.* There is a great difference between unanswered prayer and ungranted petitions. The purpose of prayer is communion and conversation with God. The period of waiting for the granting of some request is often rewarded by a far greater gift than what we asked for. The Lord himself. What is delayed or denied is according to a much greater plan and wisdom than we possess in our finite perception.

A dry spell, when it seems that the Lord has departed from us, is a sure sign that we are on the edge of a new level of depth in our relationship with the Lord. The purpose of unanswered prayer is to lead us from hearsay to heartsight.

Job could say, "I have heard of You by the hearing of the ear, but now my eye sees You."

Oswald Chambers said,

> Our understanding of God is the answer to prayer. Getting things from God is His indulgence of us. When He stops giving us things, He brings us into the place where we can begin to understand Him. As long as we get from God everything we ask for, we never get to know Him; we look at Him as a blessing machine. Your Father knows what you have need of before you ask Him. Then why pray? To get to know your Father. It is not enough to be able to say "God is love." We have to *know* that He is love. We have to struggle through until we do see His love and justice. Then our prayer is answered.*

The personal and practical application to all this is that when prayers seem unanswered, take it as a signal that the Lord wants to help us discover our sufficiency in Him and not what He can give us in tangible blessings.

When I talked with the woman who had written me the note about what seemed to her to be unanswered prayer, I discovered that she was facing physical difficulties and a breakdown of communication in her marriage. She had asked the Lord for healing and a change in her relationship with her husband. The more we talked, the more I became convinced that she needed the Lord more than she needed physical health or the change in her husband's attitude, which she had delegated the Lord to pull off for her. Prior to these difficulties her relationship with the Lord had drifted into vague blandness. Her physical and relational problems had shocked her into a realization that she needed God's help. But did she need or want God? That was the issue.

I asked a penetrating question.

"What if you are not healed and your marriage fails? Will you still want God for God?"

That alarmed her and prepared her for some deep conversation about allowing the Lord to be her ultimate and total security—for now and eternity. After several visits she was ready to surrender herself completely to the Lord's love and care. She told Him that she wanted a consistent and abiding relationship with Him more than the answer she had demanded. His Spirit entered her ready mind and heart.

Later, prayers by me and the elders of the church for her physical healing were answered. The stress that had been hindering the flow of the Lord's healing Spirit was dissipated, and she could receive what He had been willing to give all along. The woman was also ready to stop blaming her husband for all that was wrong in her marriage, and she asked the Lord to change their marriage beginning with her.

When she let up on her criticism and complaining, and became the Lord's person in her marriage, her husband was amazed at what was happening to his wife. Because she had surrendered him and his attitudes to the Lord, her efforts to change him were replaced by an effort to be to him the love and forgiveness the Lord was increasingly becoming to her. Eventually, when he could no longer blame his wife for the problems in their marriage, he was motivated to get help with his own attitudes. A Christian counselor put him through the paces of marriage counseling, which resulted in a radical personality transformation. Though he had been a member of the church and active in the program, he too had not known the Lord personally. The counselor completed his program of helping him by leading him through a prayer of commitment and a willingness to receive the Holy Spirit as the power to implement what he had discovered about what it meant to love and care for his wife.

What the woman had called an unanswered prayer when she first appealed for help was really not a denial of her prayers but the Lord's wise delay. He did answer, but in a so much greater way than she had dared to anticipate. The Lord answered first with himself, then with spiritual healing of her soul, and finally a solution beyond her expectation.

Not Ready to Receive

This leads us to the second thing the Lord wants to teach us in times in which we feel He has not answered our prayers. The woman I've described asked for help but was not ready to receive what the Lord was willing to give. Now we must consider unanswered prayers for things that *may not be best for us or are not in keeping with the Lord's timing for us.* When I think of some of my "unanswered" prayers, I am filled with thanksgiving.

A good example of this in my life has been the way the Lord led me into a national television ministry. Several years ago I thought I knew exactly what I should do. I devised a format for a program that featured interviews and performances by Christian stars and leaders with a very brief, closing meditation done by me at the end. Three pilot programs were completed featuring people like Jimmy Stewart, Carol Lawrence, and Dale Evans and Roy Rogers. Not a bad billing for success. But efforts to raise money for a full series and syndication seemed blocked at every turn. Even though a large company in America offered to be sponsor, the networks were reluctant to run a "religious" program on prime time. Since the company wanted only a network program, that possibility was lost. Other schemes of syndication were tried with little response. Even those who turned down the program could not explain why.

All the time I was praying and disturbed by what appeared to me to be no answer from the Lord. Finally, I cried out, "What's wrong, Lord? Where have I missed in what I thought was Your plan for me?" Silence for weeks. Then one day I received a series of phone calls from trusted friends. One of them spoke clearly the same thought all the others had tried to communicate. "Lloyd," he said, "you've spent all your life allowing the Lord to teach you how to preach the Bible for people's deepest needs. Don't spend time on television interviewing and featuring famous names. Just do what you do best—talk to people about their hopes and hurts and introduce them to the abundant and eternal life in Christ. I was praying about you this morning and aching over your period of unanswered prayer and suddenly I felt a rush of inspiration about your need. It was so strong, I wrote it down. What came to me is what I've shared with you. I may be off base, but pray about it and see if the Lord confirms it in your own heart and mind."

That phone call led me into an experiment. I gave up the plans of the program I had wanted to do so urgently. I let go of it completely. A few days later, a man in my congregation went to the business manager of my church and gave him a check for a pilot for a very different kind of format. He said the money could be used only if I preached as the main focus of a half-hour format. His specifications perfectly matched the guidance my friend had expressed on the phone. I exclaimed with assurance, "Sometimes the Lord gives and takes away, but in this case He took away and gave back—what He wanted all along."

The pilot production confirmed the new direction. Commitment to broadcast portions of the church's worship, including the sermon and music, was affirmed by the Lord in a gift through a will. The woman who had left the money had specifically directed that it should be used for expanding the pastor's communication of the gospel. It was just enough for the first 13 weeks' cost of production and airing on a local Los Angeles station.

Now years later, as the program reaches over 300 cities in America, I look back at the goodness of the Lord in denying one prayer so He could give me a different strategy.

Let's Not Play God

A final thing I want to say about what seems to be unanswered prayer is a word of caution. Like Job's friends, sometimes *we play God in other people's lives by suggesting that all unanswered prayer is caused by some sin in their lives.* This is simplistic and leads to defensive self-incrimination. The result is that people usually blame themselves and seldom seek the Lord himself as the ultimate answer to all prayer. To be sure, God often delays an answer until He has prepared us to be ready for the blessing He has ready.

Our responsibility is not to accuse people of sin as an explanation of why their prayers seem not to be answered. Rather, if a person suggests that may be the cause we can ask, "Tell me, what do you think may be standing in the way?" If, in response, some sin is confessed, we are to help a person tell God about that and help him receive and know His forgiveness. Often that breaks the bind and he can be open to the Lord's answer.

The danger comes when we think we can ever be pure enough to deserve God's answers. We've all known times when the Lord has helped us when we least deserved it. Petulant perfectionism is boldly contradicted by those times when He uses us to help others know or grow in Him while we still have problems in our own lives. We can empathize with people's needs because we are acutely aware of our own.

So when our prayers seem unanswered, yes, let's ask ourselves if there is a practice, habit, relationship, or misconception that may be blocking the flow of the Lord's Spirit in us. But also, let's remember we will never be good enough to earn either salvation or the gifts the Lord longs to give us. If we could be, the Cross would not have been necessary.

God wants us to know Him more profoundly than ever. When we feel our prayers are not answered according to our specifications and timing, that feeling is really a longing for God and not just for what He can give or do for us. Thank God for those times. By them we know we have been called into a much more intimate relationship than we've ever known before.

*Oswald Chambers, source unknown.

From **Praying with Power,** by Lloyd John Ogilvie. Copyright © 1983, Regal Books, Ventura, CA 93006. Used by permission.

Chapter 9

Praise in Prayer

by Derek Prime

Background Scripture: Acts 4:23-31; Philippians 4:4-7

PRAYER is not just a matter of asking God for something. As Thomas Watson, the 17th-century Puritan, quaintly put it, "Many [who pray] have tears in their eyes, and complaints in their mouths, but few have harps in their hand, blessing and glorifying God."

Prayer Itself Is Praise

To pray to God is to praise Him. In prayer—even when I am not specifically praising God by spending time thinking about one of His attributes—I am acknowledging God as the One who is supremely worthy of my trust, and uniquely powerful to help me.

Let's imagine that I contract a serious illness. My own doctor declares himself unable to advise or help, but recommends specialists who may be able to assist. After much

enquiry and searching, I hear of a leading specialist in the relevant field of medicine, and immediately I place myself in his hands. Now without my uttering any compliments to him, my action constitutes praise of the doctor concerned. My trust in him indicates my assessment of his competence and worth.

True prayer is in itself part of our praise of God. We go to Him in a way we go to no one else. He is able to help us as no one else can.

I remember a father telling me, with considerable joy, how his daughter—in her middle 20s—had come into his study one evening and poured out to him her distress over a personal relationship that had gone wrong. His pleasure was not, of course, in his daughter's distress, but in the fact that she felt so assured of his love and concern that she could unburden herself freely and find relief through his understanding. Without saying a word about him, she was nevertheless praising him as a father—she was acknowledging what a good father she knew him to be. When we pour out our hearts to God in prayer, in a way we can do with no one else, we are praising God, we are telling Him what an incomparably good Father we know He is.

Proper Starting Points

Praise prompts prayer, or gets prayer started, something like the choke of a car. I love the account in the Book of Acts of the apostles' reaction when they were commanded not to speak or teach at all in the name of Jesus. They answered, "We cannot help speaking about what we have seen and heard" (Acts 4:20). Further threats were made to them and they were released. Immediately they went back to their own people and reported all that the chief priests and elders had said to them. Now perhaps the instinctive reaction today, if we were instructed not to preach about Jesus, would be to call a committee meeting or a seminar for consultation among Christian leaders. But the early Christians convened a prayer meeting.

Notice their starting point: " 'Sovereign Lord,' they said, 'you made the heaven and the earth and the sea, and everything in them. You spoke by the Holy Spirit through the mouth of your servant, our father David: "Why do the nations rage and the peoples plot in vain? The kings of earth take their stand and the rulers gather together against the Lord and against his Anointed One" ' " (Acts 4:24-26).

They began by recalling God's *sovereignty* and *almighty power* both in creation and in the affairs of men. In other words, they began not with their immediate situation but with God himself. But how effectively their praise of God related to their situation! With God on the throne, and His power available to all who honour His Son and do His will, they went on to ask, "Now, Lord, consider their threats and enable your servants to speak your word with great boldness. Stretch out your hand to heal and perform miraculous signs and wonders through the name of your holy servant Jesus" (Acts 4:29-30). Far from asking God to stop the hindrances, they asked Him to use them to advance His purposes. No wonder Luke is able to record, "After they prayed, the place where they were meeting was shaken. And they were all filled with the Holy Spirit and spoke the word of God boldly" (v. 31).

God answered their prayers. While it is not normal for God to give such unusual signs of answering prayer, it is still true that as His people praise Him by making His glory the starting point of their prayers, it is His prerogative to give uncommon signs of His presence when He knows that that is the precise encouragement or deliverance His people need in some seemingly desperate situation.

Seeing Things Straight

Praise also enables us to pray with a proper perspective. I expect many of us have had the experience of becoming extremely upset about a situation, and afterward laughing at ourselves that we allowed it to happen. In my own experience, this kind of thing happens when I forget to praise God for His *past* goodness to me. What happens is that something goes wrong in my life, and I so easily panic. I imagine the worst possible course of events must follow, and all appears black. I then make not only myself miserable but others too.

But that situation may be avoided if I begin by pondering God's past dealings with me, and all that He is to me now in Jesus Christ. So instead of saying, "How on earth am I going to get through this?" I begin by saying to God, "I thank You for all You have been to me in *the past,* and I praise You *now* that Your grace in Jesus Christ is more than sufficient for this new situation, and I dare to pray that You may be praised by means of it, as I demonstrate what You can mean to an ordinary person like myself."

Perhaps the word *thanksgiving* in Philippians 4:6 should be underlined by us: "Do not be anxious about anything, but in everything, by prayer and petition, *with thanksgiving,* present your requests to God." And, significantly, the exhortation is prefaced by another: "Rejoice in the Lord always. I will say it again: Rejoice!" (v. 4). The reminder that no matter how my circumstances change the Lord does not change, and that He has been my constant Deliverer, calls forth renewed praise—whatever my circumstances—and provides a proper perspective as I pray, for I ask Him then with confidence to renew His kindness to me.

When Martin Luther was in the depths of despair, his wife took the rather bold and dramatic step of dressing herself in black, so that he asked, "Who has died?" Her reply was that by his behaviour he gave the impression that God had. This rebuke was enough to arouse him to the renewed exercise of faith, and praise to God. God lives! And His Son Jesus Christ rose from the dead and is at God's right hand *for us.* Praise places our needs in the perspective of God's power and grace.

The Place of Silence

Praise in prayer need not always be expressed in words —whether spoken in the heart or by the lips. It may be a prayer too deep for words. There is a place, therefore, for silence in our coming before God. We praise Him when we simply wait silently before Him. "Be still, and know that I am God," the Lord instructs (Psalm 46:10). "The Lord is in his holy temple; let all the earth be silent before him," urges Habakkuk (2:20). Here, as elsewhere, there is "a time to be silent and a time to speak" (Ecclesiastes 3:7). Since God hears without words, through silence we may talk to Him. Because God can read our hearts more easily than we can read a book, God hears without our putting our feelings always into words.

One night George Whitefield, the great 18th-century evangelist, preached with such power and evidences of God working in people's lives, that he could scarcely speak any more because of his sense of awe. "After I came home," he wrote in his journal, "I threw myself upon the bed, and in awful silence admired the infinite freedom, sovereignty, and condescension of the love of God." Silence provides the soul with scope and opportunity to ponder God's greatness.

To be able to sit in silence and enjoy another person's company is a mark of deep and true friendship. A love that has no silence sometimes has no depth in it. Observe, for example, a loving mother watching her children as they romp and play close by. Or watch a young man who has just become engaged, looking at his fiancée as she comes into the room. Their eyes—and their silence—may say more than their words.

Silence has another importance: There are things we do not hear unless we are silent. Where I live, we can sometimes hear the foghorns on the vessels that go up and down the Firth of Forth. But we hear them usually first thing in the morning and late at night. It is not that they sound only then, but that we are only quiet then. Most of us live with what often can be the nuisance of noise. In moments of silent prayer, when by the attitude of our heart we express our praise of God, we may find Him working in our lives and enabling us to discern His voice in ways we would otherwise miss.

A weaned child gives unspoken praise to its mother as it rests content and satisfied in her arms. David wrote, "I have stilled and quieted my soul; like a weaned child with its mother, like a weaned child is my soul within me" (Psalm 131:2). We praise God by relaxing in His presence as our Heavenly Father who accepts us because we are His sons and daughters by a wonderful act of adoption.

Use the Choke

Perhaps we need to pull out the "spiritual choke" of praise in prayer much more than we do. Certainly that's true for myself. If we compile our list of God's attributes in our prayer diary, with helpful scriptures placed against each, this will certainly assist us. Equally helpful—and sometimes even more stimulating—is to read the Scriptures with the deliberate endeavour to lay hold of truths they teach about God himself, and for which I can praise Him.

The best way for me to illustrate this method is perhaps not to choose obvious passages but two passages that I have read today in the course of my daily reading. The first was Psalm 93, and as I read it in the *New International Version* I noted words and phrases that speak of God himself: "The Lord reigns, he is robed in majesty; . . . armed with strength. . . . Your throne was established long ago; you are from all eternity. . . . the Lord on high is mighty. . . . holiness adorns your house for endless days" (vv. 1-2, 4-5). Notice how many attributes of God just tumble out, one after another in this one psalm: God's sovereignty, majesty, strength, eternity, might, and holiness. My heart soon responded as I meditated upon these features of God's character, and I found myself responding in praise. Praise then moved to prayer as I asked God for strength for today and God's might to achieve holiness in my life.

The other passage, totally different, was Acts 16:6-34, which begins with Paul's vision of the man of Macedonia, his arrival with Silas and perhaps others in Philippi, and the conversion of Lydia and the Philippian jailer—the latter after Paul and Silas were thrown in prison unjustly for being instrumental in delivering a slave girl from an evil spirit. It was not difficult to look at the passage from the point of view of God's attributes, and with the desire to praise Him. First, God's power to guide His servants stands out (vv. 6-12). Second, God's grace in opening a woman's heart to respond to Paul's message (v. 14). Third, God's power to deliver men and women from Satan (v. 18), and His servants from prison (v. 26). And fourth, God's saving grace in our Lord Jesus Christ so freely extended to all who believe (vv. 30-34). Once again, the offering of praise prompted prayer: prayer for guidance, the opening of people's hearts to the gospel, the salvation of men and women from Satan's power, the deliverance of God's servants in prison, and the conversion of whole families.

If we begin by praising God in our prayers, there is little doubt that we will end up as we should. We will both pray correctly and end by praising Him all the more. To this end we were created.

From **Created to Praise,** by Derek Prime. Copyright © 1981, Hodder and Stoughton Limited, London, England. Used by permission.

Chapter 10

Praying Together: The Benefits

by Larry W. White

Background Scripture: Acts 2:1-4, 42-47; Romans 12:1-2

I HATED IT! I mean, I really hated it! Yet I had no choice, I had to go. I knelt at that church altar for what seemed like hours, shifting my weight from one knee to another, wondering if I would ever be able to stand again, and certain I would have bruises on both knees.

All this because of old Mr. Nielson. You know the kind of fellow I mean; you had someone just like him in your church, too. He took seriously the commandment to "pray without ceasing," and he practiced it in every midweek prayer service.

As I look back on this scene, I realize that those midweek prayer meetings were not quite as horrible as I thought. In fact, they helped me begin to shape my attitude toward group prayer, and even individual prayer. It has taken me a long time to begin to really appreciate group prayer, and to experience its value for myself. Even today, I'm still very much a beginner, and I hope I'm always a learner. However, I'd like to invite you on an adventure to discover the benefits and joys of group prayer.

The Benefit of Community

How does a person realize most fully that he is part of a family? Isn't it when the family gets together? The church family is a community—a group of people who come together around a common interest, the person of Jesus Christ. So it is in a church's gathering that there is an obvious sense of Jesus in the midst. The Lord said, "Where two or three come together in my name, there am I with them."

"At this point in the service, National Headquarters suggests we recite 'The Lord's Prayer' in Chinese."

As we come together around the person of Jesus and are being united with God, the Father, we also become united with each other. The greater our sense of unity with the Father, the greater our unity with each other, and the greater our awareness of being a family—a real community. We can take this a step further and say, the greater our unity, the greater our ability to be conscious of God, which is a primary goal of prayer. Small prayer groups can be a vehicle for the intense development of community.

The Benefit of Spiritual Transformation

Let me ask this question: Have you noticed a connection between your thought patterns and your character? I believe that if you will take time to evaluate this, you will discover that what you think about, you become. The writer of the Proverbs said that as a man "thinketh in his heart, so is he" (23:7, KJV).

I would like to make this point: If we hold God in our mind, we will be transformed by Him. If we hold the things of the world in our mind, we will become conformed to them. Remember Paul's words to the church at Rome: "Do not conform any longer to the pattern of this world, but be transformed by the renewing of your mind" (Romans 12:2). Transformation starts at the level of our conscious thinking.

Now, in the dynamic of God's presence, as we gather in prayer, it is reasonable to believe that spiritual transformation will take place. That transformation will take in the whole group. We will discover that God, by the power of His Spirit, will begin to make us more like Him. And this spiritual growth is not only individual but also corporate. The entire group will grow.

Let's look at Acts 2 for a model. We are told in the first verse that the believers were in one place and of one mind. It was in that atmosphere that God poured out His Spirit upon them. As we read on, there can be no doubt that this group was transformed. We are told in the last verses of chapter 2 that they continued gathering together in study, prayer, and fellowship. In doing this, they allowed God to continue the growth process in them.

E. Stanley Jones once wrote: "Thoughts are motor, they move from mind to heart to action." Paul confirms this in Philippians 4:8-9 when he writes: "Finally, brothers, whatever is true, whatever is noble, whatever is right, whatever is pure, whatever is lovely, whatever is admirable—if anything is excellent or praiseworthy—think about such things. Whatever you have learned or received or heard from me, or seen in me—put it into practice. And the God of peace will be with you."

The Benefit of Knowing God's Will

Let me make a bold assertion: It is possible for a group of Christians to know God's perfect will. Have you ever experienced it? If prayer is, in fact, as writer Albert Day says, "To set God at the center of your attention; to open yourself to the illumination of His knowledge about yourself and your situation; to create within you such sympathy for the divine interest, then it would seem we can know together His divine guidance."

Remember again the Acts 2 passage. The believers gathered in the Upper Room in prayer, and when the Day of Pentecost came they were of one mind. This seems foreign to our general experience in the church. Do you know what I believe the problem is? We are too impatient. We are not willing to stay at it long enough to allow God to strip away our individual prejudices so we can become open enough in our souls to hear what He wants to say to us.

Now I know this takes us back to old Mr. Nielson, and bruises on the knees. But listen again to what Paul wrote in Romans 12:2, "Do not conform any longer to the pattern of this world, but be transformed by the renewing of your mind." Now here's the point: "Then you will be able to test and approve what God's will is—his good, pleasing and perfect will." As group prayer can bring transformation through our minds, so it can bring an understanding of what the good and perfect will of God is, if we are willing to stay with it long enough. This is true not only of group decisions but also as we try to help an individual group member discover God's will.

Jesus said, "If two of you on earth agree about anything you ask for, it will be done for you by my Father in heaven" (Matthew 18:19). Now that is POWERFUL, and the world is looking for POWER. People have been known to do almost anything to get power. Yet it is available to every Christian who will open himself to God through prayer. As believers discover God's will together in prayer, then they can unite their hearts and believe that God will answer the prayer. There is real power in corporately knowing and claiming the will of God. Can you see the real benefit to group prayer?

The Benefit of Discovering Others

While prayer opens us up to God, we also need to allow it to open us up to others. We spend so much of our lives hiding from one another. We don't let others *really* know us because to allow them into our lives makes us feel some responsibility toward them. And besides, if I let you into my life, I become vulnerable. It would open me up to the possibility of being hurt.

Prayer opens us more fully to God. It allows God greater access to our lives. When God grows in me, an amazing thing happens, I have a greater desire for intimacy. In her book, *Clinging: The Experience of Prayer* (Harper & Row), Emilie Griffen makes this profound statement: "Prayer, it seems, disposes us to friendship, in that it more and more lays us open to experience from any source, makes us sensitive to every aspect of existence, every leaf, every ray of light, every hurt, every sorrow, every pain." May I add, it makes us sensitive to every person. Now, let me move us on to the point that is crying out to be taken seriously: that is, in a small prayer group, an intimacy will grow in the Lord that will make it all right to know and to be known.

The Benefit of Healing

The words of James chapter 5 make a distinct connection between confession and healing. Let me declare that small prayer groups, under the power of the Spirit, can become healing places. I am not talking strictly of physical healing, but of emotional and spiritual healing as well. In the unity and community of the prayer group, we can hear and receive the words, "Your sins are forgiven. Go and sin no more."

I tell you, so many people need to hear the pronouncement of sins forgiven. After Jesus said to His disciples, "Receive the Holy Spirit" (John 20:22), He went on to say, "If you forgive anyone his sins, they are forgiven; if you do not forgive them, they are not forgiven." There are countless people in the church who do not feel forgiven, in part, because they have never heard anyone say, "Your sins are forgiven." This is not to say their sins are unforgiven, but it is to say they need to hear the pronouncement. Without this, many will go on living in bondage. Jesus was not saying that the disciples had power in themselves to forgive sin, but rather that they were pronouncing what Jesus had already done by way of His death and resurrection.

In an atmosphere of small-group prayer, where there is a real consciousness of God, it becomes all right to say, "I have sinned." It is a place to hear that you are forgiven. And it is a place where healing can take place.

The Benefit of Love

There is another benefit to group prayer that needs to be expressed. It really is that which ties all of this together. A unique kind of love develops among people who pray together in this openness to God. Again quoting from Emilie Griffen's book, *Clinging:* "To love another person in God is very different. . . . To love in Christ, to move and have one's being in Him, is to magnify another person, to strengthen that person, to take the other's fears and concerns as our own, to exchange places and to love her or him not only as ourselves, but even more than we love ourselves."

Again from *Clinging:* "Between Christians who pray there is a magnetic field: an attraction more powerful than any merely human passion, but like human passion. The passion of this friendship drives us to holiness. That is its distinguishing mark. Friendships in God are not found by seeking friendship, but by seeking God." This benefit brings us full circle. It brings us right back to the first benefit we discussed, development of community for which the human heart is crying.

The benefits of praying together that we have dealt with here are by no means the only ones. These are just a few I wanted to mention, in an effort to invite you to develop small-group prayer cells. Let me suggest one possible pattern for your prayer cell:

1. Ask God to lead you to the people He wishes for you to be involved with. They may or may not be people you know well.

2. Prepare a comfortable environment. A place that has a homey atmosphere is best. Perhaps some soft music playing as your prayer partners arrive will help set them at ease.

3. Sit in a circle and for the first minute or so, consider holding hands around the circle. Suggest that each person try to be aware of the others gathered in the room. Remember that God has come in each one and as you open yourself to one another, you open yourself to God.

4. Do not let words dominate your time together in prayer. Let the focus be on God rather than on the words you say.

5. Try to keep to the agreed time schedule.

Enjoy your prayer time together. It's a unique and precious gift God has given us. In a way, it's a preview of heaven.

Chapter 11

Meditative Prayer

by Richard J. Foster

Background Scripture: Psalm 19:1-14

JESUS CHRIST is alive and here to teach His people himself. His voice is not hard to hear; His vocabulary is not hard to understand. But we must learn how to hear His voice and to obey His Word; that is the heart and soul of Christian meditation.

While many biblical figures knew how to meditate, today most Christians don't even know where to begin. So we'll start with a simple description of the three basic steps into meditative prayer.

Centering Down

The first step I call "centering down." The idea is to let go of all competing distractions until we are truly centered.

Begin by seating yourself comfortably, and then slowly and deliberately let all tension and anxiety drop away. Become aware of God's presence in the room. Perhaps in your imagination you will want to visualize Christ seated in the chair across from you, for He is truly present. If frustrations or distractions arise, you will want to lift them up into the arms of the Father and let Him care for them. This is not suppressing our inner turmoil, but letting go of it. Suppression implies a pressing down, a keeping in check, whereas centering down involves giving away, releasing. More than a neutral psychological relaxing, it is an active surrendering, a "self-abandonment to divine providence," to use the phrase of Jean-Pierre de Caussade.

Because the Lord is present with us, we can relax and let go of everything, for nothing really matters, nothing is important, except attending to Him. We allow inner distractions and frustrations to melt away before Him as snow

before the sun. We allow Him to calm the storms that rage within. We allow His great silence to still our noisy hearts.

Let me warn you at the outset: in the beginning, this centeredness does not come easily or quickly. Most of us live such fractured and fragmented lives that collectedness is a foreign world to us. The moment we genuinely try to be centered we become painfully aware of how distracted we are.

But we must not be discouraged at this. We must be prepared to devote all of our meditation time to this centeredness without any thought for result or reward. We willingly "waste our time" in this manner as a lavish love offering to the Lord. For God takes what looks like a foolish waste and uses it to nudge us closer into the holy of holiness. Romano Guardini perceptively comments, "If at first we achieve no more than the understanding of how much we lack in inner unity, something will have been gained, for in some way we will have made contact with that center which knows no distraction."

Several things occur in the process of centering down. First, we surrender to Him "who is, and who was, and who is to come, the Almighty" (Revelation 1:8). We surrender control over our lives and destinies. In an act of deliberate intention, we decide to do it not our way, but God's way. We might even want to visualize our bodies being lifted into the intense light of God's presence that he may do with us as it pleases Him.

We surrender our possessiveness and invite Him to possess us in such a way that we are truly crucified with Christ and yet truly live through His life (Galatians 2:20). We relinquish into His hands our imperialist ambitions to be greater and more admired, to be richer and more powerful, even to be saintlier and more influential.

We surrender our cares and worries. "Cast all your anxiety on him because he cares for you," said Peter (1 Peter 5:7). And so we can, precisely because we sense His care. We can give up the need to watch out for number one because we have One who is watching out for us. I sometimes picture a box in which I place every worry and care. When it is full, I gift-wrap it, placing a big bow on top, and give it as a present to the Father. He receives it, and once He does, I know I must not take it back, for to take back a gift is most discourteous.

A second thing that occurs within us as we are learning to center down is the rise of a spirit of repentance and confession. As we enter the presence of a holy God, we become aware, keenly aware, of our shortcomings and many sins. All excuses are stripped away, all self-justifications silenced. A deep, godly sorrow wells up within for the things we have done and left undone. Any deed or thought that cannot stand in the searching light of Christ becomes repulsive not only to God but to us as well. Thus humbled under the Cross, we confess our need and receive His gracious word of forgiveness.

Third, as we become more and more centered, we begin to accept the ways of God with human beings. We are acutely aware that God's ways are not our ways, that His thoughts are not our thoughts. And with certainty born of fellowship, we see that His ways are altogether good. Our impatience, our rebellion, our nonacceptance give way to a gentle receptiveness to divine breathings. This is not a stoic resignation to "the will of God." It is an entering into the rhythm of the Spirit. It is a recognition that His commandments are "for our good always" (Deuteronomy 6:24, KJV). It is a letting go of our way and a saying yes to God's way—not grudgingly, but because we know it is the better way.

We might want to visualize ourselves on a secluded beach observing the footprints of God in the sand. Slowly we begin to place our feet into the prints in the sand. At some places the stride looks far too long for our small frame; at other places it looks so short that it appears childlike. In His infinite wisdom God is stretching us where we need to be on the edge of adventure, restraining us where we need greater attentiveness to Him. As we follow His lead, we enter more and more into His stride, turning where He turns, accepting His ways and finding them good.

Beholding the Lord

As we learn to center down we begin to move into the second step in meditative prayer—"beholding the Lord." By this I mean the inward, steady gaze of the heart upon the divine Center. We bask in the warmth of His presence. Worship and adoration, praise and thanksgiving well up from the inner sanctuary of the soul.

The Prayer of Listening

As we experience the unifying grace of centering down and the liberating grace of beholding the Lord, we are ushered into a third step in meditative prayer—the prayer of listening. We have put away all obstacles of the heart, all scheming of the mind, all vacillations of the will. Divine graces of love and adoration wash over us like ocean waves. As this happens, we experience an inward attentiveness to divine motions. At the center of our being we are hushed. The experience is more profound than mere silence or lack of words. There is stillness, to be sure, but it is a listening stillness. We feel more active than we ever do when our minds are frenzied. Something deep inside has been awakened and brought to attention. Our spirit is on tiptoe, alert and listening.

In meditative prayer we are growing into what Thomas à Kempis called "a familiar friendship with Jesus." We are sinking down into the light and life of Christ and becoming comfortable in that position. The perpetual presence of the Lord (omnipresence, as we say) changes from a theological dogma into a radiant reality. "He walks with me and He talks with me" ceases to be pious jargon and instead becomes a straightforward description of daily life.

I am not speaking of some mushy, giddy, buddy-buddy

relationship. Such insipid sentimentality only betrays how little we know, how distant we are from the Lord high and lifted up who is revealed to us in Scripture. John tells us in his Apocalypse that when he saw the reigning Christ, he fell at His feet as though dead, and so should we (Revelation 1:17). No, I am speaking of a reality more akin to what the disciples felt in the Upper Room when they experienced both intense intimacy and aweful reverence.

In meditative prayer we create the emotional and spiritual space that allows Christ to construct an inner sanctuary in the heart.

Seven Suggestions

Over the years I have noticed several practical concerns that always seem to surface when we actually implement meditation.

1. Falling asleep. It is a tragedy that so many of us live with the emotional spring wound so tightly that the moment we begin to relieve the tension, sleep overtakes us. The ultimate answer lies in learning to better get in touch with our bodies and our emotions. Fully alert and fully relaxed are completely compatible states. I find, however, that most of us cannot learn this in an instant. So rather than chide and condemn yourself if you find yourself falling asleep when you are trying to meditate, accept the sleep gratefully, for no doubt you need it. And you can invite the Lord to teach you and minister to your spirit while you sleep. You will discover that the problem will soon recede into the background.

2. Spiritual influences. Another concern relates to the fear of spiritual influences that are not of God. It is a good fear to have, for Scripture is clear that spiritual forces war against our soul. But the fear does not need to paralyze us, for "the one who is in you is greater than the one who is in the world" (1 John 4:4). While evil powers are great, Christ's power is greater still. And so before every experience of meditation, I offer this simple invocation for protection: "I surround myself with the light of Christ, I cover myself with His blood, and I seal myself with His cross." I know that when I do this no influence can harm me, whether emotional, physical, or spiritual, for I am protected by the strong light of Christ.

3. Wandering mind. By far the most commonly asked question relates to the problem of a wandering mind. This no doubt reflects the fractured state of modern society. We are bombarded by so many stimuli, and our schedules are piled so high with commitments that the moment we seek to enter the creative silences, every demand screams for attention. We have noisy hearts.

We can begin to deal with a wandering mind by understanding that the inner clatter is telling us something about our own distraction, and it is not wrong to give our whole meditation time to learn about our inner chaos. I have found it helpful to keep a things-to-do pad with me and simply jot down the tasks that are vying for my attention until they have all surfaced. Beyond this, we need to gently, but firmly, speak the word of peace to our racing mind and so instruct it into a more disciplined way. And if one particular matter repeatedly intrudes into our meditation, we may ask God if He wants to teach us something through the intrusion, and so befriend the intruder by making *it* the object of our meditation.

4. Place. Every place is sacred in the Lord, and we need to know that wherever we are *is* holy ground. We are a portable sanctuary and, by the power of God, we sanctify all places. But most of us find certain places more conducive to meditative prayer than others. And so we would do well to find a place of beauty that is quiet, comfortable, and free from emotional and physical distractions. With a little creativity most of us can arrange such a place (and space) with minimal effort.

I have also discovered that certain activities are particularly conducive to meditative prayer. Swimming and jogging are singularly appropriate for this interior work. Some have found gardening an ideal time to know the Lord, who made heaven and earth (Psalm 124:8). More recently I have been enjoying periods of meditation while riding the bus, and while it takes a little practice to disregard the ordinary commotion, it soon becomes a wonderful place of solitude.

5. Length. For the most part, how long you meditate depends on your past experience and internal readiness. Some have lived so frantically that 5 or 10 minutes of quietness stretches them to the limit. But in time 30 to 40 minutes should feel comfortable. I would not recommend longer than one hour at any given time. Let your own needs and abilities determine your schedule. It is better to take small portions and digest them fully than to attempt to gorge yourself and get indigestion. I have often found it helpful to have a little longer meditation on Monday to begin the week (say 30 to 40 minutes) followed by briefer morning meditations for the rest of the week (maybe 15 to 20 minutes) with brief centering meditations (no more than 5 minutes) sprinkled throughout each day.

6. Time. The best time for meditation varies from person to person and often is different for any individual at different points in his life. For example, in my high school years the morning hour was especially valuable; as a college student a free hour just before lunch met my needs better; in graduate school less frequent but more extended periods were most helpful, and in more recent years the morning time again seems best. You will find your own rhythm. Find the time when your energy level is at its peak and give that—the best of your day—to this sacred work.

7. Posture. Most of us fail to understand how helpful the body can be in spiritual work. For example, if we feel particularly distracted and out of touch with spiritual things, a consciously chosen posture of kneeling can help call the inner spirit to attention. The hands outstretched or placed on the knees palms up gently nudges the inner mind into a stance of receptivity. Slouching telegraphs inattention; sitting straight telegraphs alertness. I most often suggest sitting in a comfortable but straight chair with the back correctly positioned and both feet flat on the ground. Richard Rolle said that in "sitting I am most at rest, and my heart most upward." But again, determine what fits best for you.

The Wellspring of Meditation

Our world desperately needs people who have dared to explore the interior depths and can therefore lead us all into richer ways of living. In these inviting words, the great Japanese Christian Toyohiko Kagawa encourages each of us to experience deeply the One who offers living water: "Those who draw water from the wellspring of meditation know that God dwells close to their hearts. For those who wish to discover the quietude of old amid the hustle and bustle of today's machine civilization, there is no way save to rediscover this ancient realm of meditation. Since the loss of my eyesight I have been as delighted as if I had found a new wellspring by having arrived at this sacred precinct."

Taken from **Meditative Prayer,** by Richard J. Foster. © 1983 by Inter-Varsity Christian Fellowship of the U.S.A. and used by permission of InterVarsity Press, Downers Grove, IL 60515.

Chapter 12

When Should We Fast?

by Amy Prange

Background Scripture: Isaiah 58:1-9; Matthew 6:16-18

I ORDERED ONLY WATER at a restaurant on a trip to Florida. "What do you mean, you're fasting?" my mother asked anxiously. "Aren't you going a little overboard with Christianity?"

I'd fasted before, but never around my family, only at the dorm where I could go without food and no one would notice. Now I had to answer to Mom.

When I first fasted, I didn't know much about it. My school offered us the chance to skip dinner on Good Friday and give the money for the dinner to a hunger relief organization. At first, I decided to fast until the next morning, but on Easter morning I had my first meal in 45 hours.

All I knew at the time was that I enjoyed fasting. Never

before had Easter meant so much to me. Never had I appreciated food as a life-sustainer and nothing more. Never had I realized the truth of the words, "Man shall not live by bread alone, but by every word that proceeds from the mouth of God" (Matthew 4:4, RSV). Never had I felt so weak, yet so strong in God's provision and at peace with life.

O. Hallesby says in his book *Prayer* (Augsburg): "Fasting helps to give us that inner sense of spiritual penetration by means of which we can discern clearly that for which the Spirit of prayer would have us pray in exceptionally difficult circumstances." Fasting brings a special awareness of spiritual truth and of God. Hallesby suggests that fasting should be done especially in times of temptation, before making a big decision, and before planning or carrying out a difficult task.

Though my first fast was pleasant, I didn't know about the power of fasting, that we can fast today, as in Bible times, to gain spiritual insight and guidance, and to channel special power in times of need.

But now I know.

Fast Look at the Bible

Fasting is mentioned over 70 times in the Bible. Yet, in spite of the many references to it, fasting is one of the most neglected spiritual and physical exercises among Christians today. It is often considered a fanatical health hazard left over from medieval Christianity.

The early Christian church, probably in the second century, began to commemorate the passion of Christ by fasting until midafternoon twice a week. Christians would go without food on Wednesdays to remember our Lord's betrayal and on Fridays to remember His death. In the fourth century, during a period of persecution, the celebration of Lent began—and it is still a time of abstention from certain foods for some churches.

Puritans in Plymouth Colony in New England had regular fast days to prevent plagues, droughts, Indian attacks, disease, and other threatening disasters. Bishops in the Roman Catholic church called for days of fasting in times of misfortune as an act of penance to plead for forgiveness. When asceticism (the practice of self-denial) became common in the Catholic church, fasting was a major practice. As one ascetic wrote, "One should not ponder divine matters on a full stomach. For the well-fed, even the superficial secrets of the Trinity are hidden."

We need to reconsider the option of fasting. O. Hallesby says, "So far from the teaching of Jesus and the apostles concerning fasting have we strayed. It is no doubt high time that we feeble, weak-willed and pleasure-loving Christians begin to see what the Scriptures say concerning this element of our sanctification."

Today's doer of the Word striving to be like Christ must

determine the principles of fasting from examples and from Jesus' teachings.

Fasting is unique among biblical ideas. Unlike teaching and prophecy, it is not a gift. Unlike prayer and praise, it is not a command. Only examples of fasting are given in the Bible.

In Matthew 6:16, Jesus speaks of "when you fast." Some argue that Jesus fully expects the listener to fast because He says "when" instead of "if." However, Jesus spoke these words to a predominantly Jewish group who fasted as a religious custom. Can we conclude from this that Jesus wants *us* to fast?

Jesus himself fasted once according to the Gospels. Led by the Spirit, Jesus spent 40 days and 40 nights without food in the wilderness (Matthew 4:1-2).

The disciples probably did not fast while Jesus was on earth. "Can the wedding guests fast while the bridegroom is with them?" (Mark 2:19, RSV). Only a few sketchy examples of their fasts after the resurrection are recorded.

With so few examples in the New Testament, I turned to the Old Testament for information. There, I discovered the following occasions for fasting: (1) mourning (1 Chronicles 10:12; 1 Samuel 31:13); (2) confession and repentance (1 Samuel 7:6; Joel 1:14); (3) intercession for God to suspend His judgments of persons or towns (Jeremiah 36:9; Jonah 3:5); (4) quest for wisdom or insight (2 Chronicles 20:3; Judges 20:26); (5) request for protection and safe journeys (Ezra 8:21; Esther 4:16); (6) worship (Nehemiah 9:1); (7) intercession for the deliverance of captives and bringing of justice (Isaiah 58:3). Sometimes God imposed an involuntary fast to teach His people (Deuteronomy 8:3; Hosea 2:8-9).

These varied occasions for fasting mentioned in the Old Testament are all pleas to God—often desperate, always sincere. Fasting showed God the earnestness of the people.

When You Fast

There are different kinds of fasts. The most common kind is abstaining from food but not from liquids. The second is going without water and food for short periods of no more than three days. There are two exceptions—Moses fasted for 80 days in God's presence, and Elijah traveled across the desert for 40 days without provisions.

Along with examples of fasts, God gives us guidelines on how not to fast. Motivations must not be self-centered. The personal benefits of fasting, such as peace and insight, often outweigh the importance of fasting to God. Isaiah speaks of the people wondering why God does not notice their fast. God replies, "Is such the fast that I choose, a day for a man to humble himself? . . . Is not this the fast that I choose: to loose the bonds of wickedness, to undo the thongs of the yoke? . . . Is it not to share your bread with the hungry, and bring the homeless poor into your house?" (Isaiah 58:5-7, RSV).

Individuals, churches, and campus fellowships sometimes fast to raise money for world hunger organizations. Such fasts increase awareness of what it is like to be without food.

When I fast, I sometimes get caught up in focusing on good deeds rather than on God. Instead of being humbled by my fast, I sometimes pride myself in it and begin to think I'm special because of my self-imposed "suffering." I too often buffet my body thinking, sometimes unconsciously, that I can merit God's favor through my fast. God's grace is free, yet it is easy to try to atone for my own sins, forgetting Christ has already paid the price.

Jesus also warns of the hypocrites who "disfigure their faces that their fasting may be seen by men" (Matthew 6:16, RSV). He says a fast should not be advertised to others but should be done in secret. It is all too easy to let fasting become an act of righteousness used to impress others with our spirituality.

108

Feast or Famine?

The Bible gives examples and guidelines for fasting, but how can we apply them? We must let the Holy Spirit be our guide, search the Scriptures, and seek counsel from people who fast and those who don't.

A word of warning: Fasting is a potentially dangerous activity. As with anything used to excess or without discretion, fasting may be harmful. Pregnant women, underweight people, and those with heart ailments, health problems, or on medication should probably not fast at all.

Opinions on the physiological effects of fasting differ greatly. Arthur Wallis, in *God's Chosen Fast,* says that after a prolonged fast you will have "a brightness of eye, pure breath, clear skin and a sense of physical well-being" due to the purging of wastes from the body and soul.

But Jacqueline Dupont, chairperson of the food and nutrition department at Iowa State University, disagrees. "Fasting is definitely not curative," she says, and because there is no accumulation of "bad" wastes, fasting only rids the body of wastes from food eaten the day before the fast.

Usually, your body goes through four stages during a prolonged fast; symptoms differ slightly from person to person. For the first two or three days, your body craves food. Then it becomes weak, and you may feel faint for two or three days. After that stage, strength increases, without hunger, until all waste products are eliminated. Starvation begins any time between the 20th and 40th day when the body begins to feed off living cells. Hunger pangs begin again, and, if the fast is carried beyond this point, serious damage may occur.

If you decide to fast, here are a few warnings and suggestions: (1) Don't fast for longer then a few days unless you are under the watchful eye of a doctor and are well-versed in the dos and don'ts of fasting. (2) Don't exercise strenuously while fasting, but exercise regularly, except when extremely weak. (3) Don't jump into prolonged fasts. Allow your body time to adjust, starting with one- or two-day fasts.

Though biblical guidance on fasting may seem incomplete, fasting should not be ignored. It can help us keep a balance in our lives. Richard Foster writes, "How easily we begin to allow nonessentials to take precedence in our lives. How quickly we crave things we do not need until we are enslaved by them . . . Our human cravings and desires are like a river that tends to overflow its banks; fasting helps keep them in their proper channel."

Study for yourself, and discover whether God wants you to take the forgotten option.

Reprinted by permission of **HIS,** student magazine of Inter-Varsity Christian Fellowship, © 1983.

Chapter 13

The Prayer of Relinquishment

by Catherine Marshall

Background Scripture: Matthew 26:36-46

IN THE FALL of 1943 I had then been ill for six months
with a widespread lung infection, and a bevy of specialists
seemed unable to help. Persistent prayer, using all the faith
I could muster, had resulted in—nothing. I was still in bed
full time.

One afternoon a pamphlet was put in my hands. It was
the story of a missionary who had been an invalid for eight
years. Constantly she had prayed that God would make her
well, so that she might do His work. Finally, worn out with
futile petition, she prayed, "All right. I give up. If You want
me to be an invalid, that's Your business. Anyway, I want You
even more than I want health. You decide." In two weeks the
woman was out of bed, completely well.

This made no sense to me, yet I could not forget the story. On the morning of September 14—how can I ever forget the date?—I came to the same point of abject acceptance. "I'm tired of asking," was the burden of my prayer. "I'm beaten, finished. God, You decide what You want for me."

Tears flowed. I felt no faith as I understood faith, expected nothing. The gift of my sick self was made with no trace of graciousness.

And the result? It was as if I had touched a button that opened windows in heaven; as if some dynamo of heavenly

power began flowing, flowing. Within a few hours I had experienced the presence of the living Christ in a way that wiped away all doubt and revolutionized my life. From that moment my recovery began.

Through this incident and others that followed, God was trying to teach me something important about prayer. Gradually, I saw that a demanding spirit, with self-will as its rudder, blocks prayer. I understood that the reason for this is that God absolutely refuses to violate our free will; that therefore, unless self-will is voluntarily given up, even God cannot move to answer prayer.

In time, I gained more understanding about the prayer of relinquishment through the experiences of others, both in contemporary life and through books. Jesus' prayer in the Garden of Gethsemane, I came to see, is the pattern for us. Christ could have avoided the Cross. He did not have to go up to Jerusalem the last time. He could have compromised with the priests, bargained with Caiaphas. Pilate wanted to release Him, all but begged Him to say the right words that would let him do so. Even in the Garden on the night of the betrayal, Christ had plenty of time to flee. Instead He used His free will to turn the decision over to His Father.

The Phillips translation of the Gospels brings Jesus' prayer into special focus: "Dear Father . . . all things are possible to you. Let me not have to drink this cup! Yet it is not what I want but what you want" (Mark 14:36, Phillips).

There is a crucial difference here between acceptance and resignation. There is no resignation in the prayer of relinquishment. Resignation says, "This is my situation, and I resign myself and settle down to it." Resignation lies down in the dust of a godless universe and steels itself for the worst.

Acceptance says, "True, this is my situation at the moment. I'll look unblinkingly at the reality of it. But I'll also open my hands to accept willingly whatever a loving Father sends." Thus acceptance never slams the door on hope.

Yet even while it hopes, our relinquishment must be the real thing—and this giving up of self-will is the hardest thing we human beings are ever called on to do.

I remember the agony of one attractive young girl, Sara B., who told me of her doubts about her engagement. "I love Jeb," she said, "and Jeb loves me. But the problem is, he drinks. Not that he's an alcoholic or anything. But the drinking is a sort of symbol of a lot of ideas he has. It keeps bothering me—enough that I wonder if God is trying to tell me to give up Jeb."

As we talked, Sara came to her own conclusion. It was that she would lose something infinitely precious if she did not follow the highest and the best that she knew. Tears glistened in her eyes as she said, "I'm going to break the engagement. If God wants me to marry Jeb, He will see that things change—about the drinking and all."

Right then, simply and poignantly, she told God of her decision. She was putting her broken dreams and her now unknown future into God's hands.

Jeb's ideas and ideals did not change, and Sara did not marry him. A year later Sara wrote me an ecstatic letter. "It nearly killed me to give up Jeb. Yet God knew that he wasn't the one for me. Recently I've met *the* man and we're to be married. Today I *really* have something to say about the wisdom and the joy of trusting God. . . ."

It's good to remember that not even the Master Shepherd can lead if the sheep do not follow Him but insist on running ahead of Him or taking side paths.

When we come right down to it, how can we make obedience real except as we give over our self-will in each of life's episodes as it unfolds—whether we understand it or not, and even if evil appears to have initiated the episode in question? That's why it should not surprise us that at the heart of the secret of answered prayer lies the law of relinquishment.

So Mrs. Nathaniel Hawthorne, wife of the famous

American author, found as she wrestled in prayer in the city of Rome one February day in 1860. Una, the Hawthorne's eldest daughter, was dying of a virulent form of malaria. The attending physician, Dr. Franco, had warned that afternoon that unless the young girl's fever abated before morning, she would die.

As Mrs. Hawthorne sat by Una's bed, her thoughts went to her husband in the adjoining room and what he had said earlier that day, "I cannot endure the alternations of hope and fear; therefore I have settled with myself not to hope at all."

But the mother could not share Nathaniel's hopelessness. Una could not, must not die. This daughter strongly resembled her father, had the finest mind, the most complex character of all the Hawthorne children. Why should some capricious Providence demand that they give her up?

Moreover, Una had been delirious for several days, had recognized no one. Were she to die this night, there could not even be the solace of farewells.

As the night deepened, the girl lay so still that she seemed to be in the anteroom of death. The mother went to the window and looked out on the piazza. There was no moonlight; a dark and silent sky was heavy with clouds.

"I cannot bear this loss—cannot—cannot, . . ." Then suddenly, unaccountably, another thought took over. "Why should I doubt the goodness of God? Let Him take Una, if He sees best. More than that: I can *give* her to Him! I do give her to You, Lord. I won't fight against You anymore."

Then an even stranger thing happened. Having made this great sacrifice, Mrs. Hawthorne expected to feel sadder. Instead she felt lighter, happier than at any time since Una's long illness had begun.

Some minutes later she walked back to the girl's bedside, felt her daughter's forehead. It was moist and cool. Her pulse was slow and regular. Una was sleeping naturally. And the mother rushed into the next room to tell her husband that a miracle had happened.

In the realm of answered prayer the progression of events in Una's recovery was not unique. For in the years since I first read the Hawthornes' story, I keep hearing of strikingly similar experiences. This one was given me by a friend in a letter:

> ... Three years ago our son was born. At first he seemed a normal, healthy baby. But when he was not quite 12 hours old, while I was holding him in my arms for the first time, he had a convulsion. More convulsions followed in the next few days.
>
> The only explanation the doctors had was that he must have suffered a brain injury of some kind at birth. This only added to my terror. If he lived, perhaps he would be blind, deaf, dumb, or a cripple, or with his mind affected.
>
> I've never felt so alone during the time that followed. I prayed, but I couldn't feel that God cared about me anymore. Why had this had to happen to *my* baby?
>
> I know now that my prayers were not prayers at all, but accusations. I was demanding that God heal my child.
>
> Then out of sheer exhaustion of body and soul, I stopped commanding God and gave in to Him completely. I just said, "Take him if that's what You want. *Anything* You decide will be all right with me. Even if You want him to be crippled or retarded, then I will just have to learn to accept it and live with it." I put myself entirely in His hands.
>
> From that instant, not only did Larry begin to improve, but suddenly my tears left, and my fears went with them. An inexplicable peace filled my heart, and I knew, just knew that Larry would not only live but would have a normal, useful life. . . .
>
> Well, the end of the story is that Larry is now a normal and healthy little boy. He's very, very intelligent, and

if he were any more active, well, I'd be the one to be a cripple. . . .

It is obvious that Larry's story and Una's have several points in common. In each case, the mother wanted something desperately—life and health for her child. Each mother virtually commanded God to answer her prayer. While this demanding spirit had the upper hand, God seemed remote, unapproachable. Then through a combination of the obvious futility of the demanding prayer, plus weariness of body and spirit, the one praying surrendered to the possibility of what she feared most. At that instant, there came a turning point. Suddenly and unaccountably, fear left. Peace crept into the heart. There followed a feeling of lightness and joy that had nothing to do with outer circumstances. That was the turning point. From that moment, the prayer began to be answered.

Now the intriguing question is: What is the secret or spiritual law implicit in this prayer of relinquishment?

Here is part of it. . . . We know that fear is like a screen erected between us and God so that His power cannot get through to us. So, how does one get rid of fear?

This is not easy when the life of someone dear hangs in the balance, or when what we want most in all the world is involved. At such times, every emotion, every passion, is tied up in the dread of what may happen. Obviously only drastic measures can deal with such a gigantic fear and the demanding spirit that usually goes along with it. My experience has been that trying to deal with it by repeating faith affirmations is not drastic enough.

We must stop fleeing from and denying the terrible prospect. Look squarely at the possibility of what you fear most.

At the time, it seems to us that this is the opposite of trust. "Lord," we are inclined to protest, "didn't You tell us to pray with faith? I'm confused. Does relinquishment mean

117

that we can never be sure about praying for any definite thing? If it does, Lord, then how can that be faith?"

To all such pleas to understand, Jesus always patiently gives the same answer, "Obey Me. Then—after that—you will know and begin to understand."

So we take the first hard steps of obedience. And lo, as we stop hiding our eyes, force ourselves to walk up to the fear and look it full in the face—never forgetting that God and His power are still the supreme reality—the fear evaporates. Drastic? Yes. But it is one sure way of releasing prayer power into human affairs.

Sometimes the miracle of prayer gloriously answered takes place at that point. Upon occasion, God may tell us that He cannot grant us what we have asked for, as in the case of Sara B. Obviously, we have not really meant business about the prayer of relinquishment until we have faced that eventuality too.

Whenever a loving Father grants our wish, the Word appears in exterior circumstances and the miracle happens —we understand that relinquishment and faith are not contradictory. The prayer of relinquishment is the child dropping his rebellion against being a child, placing his hand in the big, protective hand of the Father, and trusting Him to lead us even in the dark.

In the prayer of faith our hand is still in His. Our heart is still obedient. But now He has led us out of the frightening darkness, with only the pressure of His hand to reassure us, into the sunlight. We look into the face beside us with a thrill of recognition—the hand of the Father is Jesus' hand!

I RELINQUISH THIS TO YOU

Father, for such a long time I have pleaded before You this, the deep desire of my heart: _____. Yet the more I've clamored for Your help with this, the more remote You have seemed.

I confess my demanding spirit in this matter. I've tried suggesting to You ways my prayer could be answered. To my shame, I've even bargained with You. Yet I know that trying to manipulate the Lord of the universe is utter foolishness. No wonder my spirit is so sore and weary!

I want to trust You, Father. My spirit knows that these verities are forever trustworthy even when I *feel* nothing. . . .

That You are there.

(You said, "Lo, I am with you always.")[1]

That You love me.

(You said, "I have loved thee with an everlasting love.")[2]

That You alone know what is best for me.

(For in You, Lord, "are hid all the treasures of wisdom and knowledge.")[3]

Perhaps all along You have been waiting for me to give up self-effort. At last I want You in my life even more than I want _____. So now, by an act of my will, I relinquish this to You. I will accept Your will, whatever that may be. Thank You for counting this act of my will as the decision of the real person even when my emotions protest. I ask You to hold me true to this decision. To You, Lord God, who alone are worthy of worship, I bend the knee with thanksgiving that this too will "work together for good."[4] *Amen.*

1. Matthew 28:20, KJV
2. Jeremiah 31:3, KJV
3. Colossians 2:3, KJV
4. Romans 8:28, KJV